Under the Locust Trees

Stories from a Kentucky Childhood
by
Dorothy Russell DeGraffenreid

For Children and former Children
Ages 10 to 110

1st Printing 1994
2nd Printing 1995
3rd Printing 2012

Table of Contents

ELOPEMENT 1920'S STYLE 1

OUR LITTLE HOUSE IN THE GARDEN 21

MYSTERIES OF BIRTH, DEATH, AND ELECTRICITY 33

WINTER AND BOUQUETS OF LACE 49

THE LITTLE GREY CABIN BEHIND THE PINK ROSES 67

UNCLE TOM LOST 93

MY FIRST AIRPLANE SIGHTINGS 125

THE DAY MARVIN SAVED ANNA LORENE'S LIFE 131

MY PLAYHOUSE UNDER THE ROAD 137

MICE IN THE WHEAT 143

MY FRIEND ANN 147

RAINBOWS AND DREAMS 165

POOLE REFLECTIONS 169

ABOUT THE FAMILY 172

Acknowledgements 174

DEDICATION

This book is dedicated to my parents, Alvie & Edna Russell, whose five children all agree that they are in that ultimate realm of best parents in the world.

PREFACE

My original purpose for these stories was to store them in a box, in the attic, along with my genealogy records. I wanted to pass on to our descendants, especially the children of the future, what kind of people we were, and how we lived in rural Kentucky in the early 1900's.

I didn't intend for these writings to be read until my 100th birthday in 2032. Then not as many people would still be around to protest if I made them look bad. This secret first leaked out during a conversation with my nephew, Dr. Mark Russell, about family history. When my oldest son Bob learned about the stories, he printed booklets for the family to read. This circulation created a demand for more.

I first planned only to make the stories factual and informative, but my humor kept getting in the way, and it put a different slant on things.

The stories are intended to be lighthearted and humorous. If anyone interprets anything in my book differently than I do, and is offended in any way, I apologize.

The sources for the events are from my memory and the memories of other members of the family. Sometimes people can have different versions of the same event. The few times a discrepancy arose, I used the version that had the most voices in agreement. I have gone to great lengths to validate my material and make it as true as possible.

Since I have only begun to crack the door into the adventure of writing, I like to compare my book to the homespun quality of a country woman's patchwork quilt. I used a pen to stitch together many small pieces of our lives, and then added a few splashes of Kentucky dialect of that era for extra color.

In spite of the rough edges, I hope these stories will warm your heart and spark memories of your own.

ATTICS

Realms of mystery
where ghosts live
and lifetimes sleep.

Waiting...waiting...waiting
for future generations.
Treasured clutter waiting
for its resurrection.

By the slip of a tongue
my secret little book
escaped this fate to wait...
and wait...and wait.

INTRODUCTION

It has been nearly 40 years since I moved away from my beloved Kentucky, but I have never forgotten the happy childhood I enjoyed there. I have not forgotten my hometown and the kind, courteous, soft-spoken, good hearted people who lived there.

A way of life in Kentucky, and my childhood, have both disappeared over the horizon, with many past sunsets. I want to preserve these stories that still live in my memory, for future generations to enjoy.

When Daniel Boone, the famous hunter and explorer, first saw Kentucky in 1769, he described it as a piece of the Garden of Eden. After he had lived there for years, he said, "Heaven must be a Kentucky kind of place." I agree, and I should know, since I lived there during most of my first 20 years, sheltered in its peaceful, protective hills.

The idea for my title came from a long row of tall locust trees that were part of the literal roots planted in Kentucky by my great grandfather, Henry Brown, after he and his mother came from North Carolina in 1869. He purchased a three acre plot near other families from the same region of North Carolina. The Civil War had destroyed their prosperous, comfortable plantation life and forced them farther West, where land was cheaper.

Although Elizabeth Rountree Brown returned to North Carolina, she came back to Kentucky in the 1890's and made it her home until her death in 1909.

Many years later, in 1922, the Russells bought this same three acres of land and Henry Brown's former blacksmith shop near the center of Poole, Kentucky.

Six generations of the Brown and Russell families have worked, rested, or played in the shade of those beautiful locust trees. They stood majestically for all those years, giving off the fragrance of their blossoms in the spring and looking like giant bouquets of lace when their bare branches were covered with snow in the winter.

They were there when Daddy brought my mother as a young bride to live in their first home. They were there when my brothers, sisters, and I were born.

The roots that kept the steep bank from washing into the ditch along old Highway 41 also served as steps at each corner of the yard. In late afternoon the leaves made a quivering, lacy pattern on the floors when the sunlight fell through an open door or window. I remember waking in the middle of the night when I was very young and seeing this pattern made by the moonlight on the varnished plank floor of the front bedroom. I slipped from the covers to sit in the middle of this magic place.

I can still feel the cool night breeze coming through the screen door and hear the gentle rustling of the leaves. I knew how a little fairy must have felt when she came out of hiding to dance in the moonbeams knowing no one was awake to see her.

The compound leaves with their rows of different sized circular leaflets provided coins for the little folded paper coin purse my great Aunt Tina taught me to make.

My first and only love kissed me goodnight under those branches when he brought me home after our dates, and I came back to that house a bride just as my mother had done. In the shade of those trees, on the front porch, I sang lullabies to my first baby. He and Jimmie's sons Junior and Larry were the last in the Brown line to live there.

Years after we moved away, someone who lived there thought a wall of large rocks would hold the bank better than the tree roots and he had a bulldozer take out the five trees in front of the house. When I heard of this, a pain smashed into my chest. In future years if I need to have my heart examined, a doctor studying the xrays is going to be very puzzled at the tiny markings across my heart that resemble bulldozer tracks.

While growing up in the town of Poole, population 250 (originally named Poole's Mill), I was always eager for the changes progress brought: the telephone, the radio, cars and paved roads, the refrigerator and washing machine, etc. But in our excitement, we failed to notice a happy way of life being trampled on and pushed aside in the process.

So much that was good has been lost. We had a slowpaced life that allowed us time to smell the flowers. We had large, extended families nearby. Grandparents, aunts, uncles, and cousins lived next door, around the corner, or just beyond the next hill. We had such a sense of safety that almost no one bothered to lock doors.

In the mornings we awoke to air so sweet and fresh we wanted to drink it. The clear, cool water from our wells was so sparkling clean we did drink it.

Then there was the space, large yards, and behind them lay pastures, corn fields, and woods as far as the eye could see in every direction.

Being by nature a curious and nosy little girl, I inspected every nook and cranny of this wonderful little world. My explorations took me from the creek bottoms to the top floor of the mill, from cellar floors to attics. I climbed into hay lofts in the barns and slid down haystacks in the fields.

Since I had many relatives and friends in town, I was able to visit inside most of the houses. Of the more than 60 houses during that period, I was in all but three and slept in many of them.

I loved the wonderful old houses. Some were already very old when I came along in 1932. They ranged from Victorian and Colonial styles with eight or ten rooms and two to four porches down to two room shacks. Most houses had fireplaces and featherbeds, a front porch and porch swing, and a water well with a gourd dipper. Most families had their own garden, cow, and chickens.

I wondered how old the beautiful houses were and who built them. I wondered what tales those old flower papered walls could tell if they could talk.

Looking back now from the vantage point of my 60th year, I realize I have stories of my own to tell. Those old walls are still not talking, but I am. So settle down in a comfortable chair while I open a dusty old trunk in the attic of my brain. I will loosen a couple of faded ribbons and let a few stories spill across the pages of this book.

If you want to read a book filled with high adventure, sex, and violence, put this one back on the shelf. But if you like country life and stories that would go with the scenes that inspired Norman Rockwell and Grandma Moses to paint, then keep reading.

These are true stories woven with many short ones that are like the scraps of lace in Mama's sewing box - too short to be good for anything, yet too good to throw away.

The setting for these stories was one of the most peaceful places on earth. No wars were ever fought there. We never had street gangs, drugs, or shootouts with police and criminals. The nearest I ever came to being caught in anything resembling a crossfire was when I sat in front of an open window in church while the scent of honeysuckles and roses floated in as the sound of singing floated out.

This book is mostly about my childhood and me, but it will begin with the elopement and marriage of my parents, because without them there would be no me.

We will take a peek, through the eyes of a young, inquisitive girl, into a little town in Kentucky during the peaceful days of long ago.

I may have overstated this tranquil stuff a teeny bit. Life was not always a bed of roses and still waters, as you will soon see.

Painting of the Brown farm by Malcolm Arnett - circa 1960

ELOPEMENT 1920'S STYLE

Springtime had come to the rolling hills of Webster County, Kentucky, in the year 1926. The daffodils we called Easter flowers were in bloom. A tinge of green was spreading across treetops in the woods that were already filled with chirping birds and small furry animals. But Mother Nature had not yet won all her yearly battles with Old Man Winter.

A chill March wind blew down the valley from the west, then spread upward across a barren corn field to the crest of a low hill. Here the cold wind helped the swelling buds push the last of the oak leaves from the tall trees in the front yard of a white clapboard farmhouse. The brittle leaves tumbled across the big yard toward the corn crib and rail fence around the horse lot.

In spite of the cold air and a grey sky heavy with a threat of snow, four young people stood on the long, low front porch. Farmer Brown's daughter, Edna Lorene, had three visitors that Sunday afternoon after church: her beau, William Alvie Russell, and their best friends, Herman and Fannie Johnson.

Herman and Fannie were newlyweds. As they stepped onto the running board of their car and said their goodbyes, they were congratulated again on their marriage the Saturday before, but were told nothing of the secret plans of the other couple.

Alvie and Edna watched and waved as the car turned toward the narrow lane and disappeared from view between the south woods and the barn. Then they hurriedly opened the door to get back to the warmth of the parlor fire.

The house had two front doors, one for each of the two large rooms in the front of the house. The room on the right was the parents' bedroom. It had two double beds in the corners opposite the fireplace, plus a dresser. Rocking chairs placed in front of the fire allowed the room to double as a sitting room.

The parlor on the left held the organ, a table and lamp, more rockers, and a fold down bed. This bed looked like a tall varnished wardrobe when it was up. At night the parlor became a bedroom when the bed was opened. Each room had a fireplace that was connected to a central chimney.

A partial view of the narrow lane.

Although the house was swarming with children, Alvie and Edna managed to whisper their final plans for their elopement. "Meet me under the big tree behind the horse lot at 1:00 A.M." he said. "And don't go to sleep." She smiled because she knew there was no danger of that; she was too excited.

They were finally going to go through with it. The opportunity had come that Friday when her brothers came home from school and announced they had taken their finals. There was still a week of school and Papa wouldn't be suspecting anything yet because the boys were dependent on their big sister for their meals and clean clothes to stay in school. Edna knew that with their tests over it wouldn't hurt them to miss the last week.

The announcement this afternoon had caught Alvie by surprise and slightly unprepared, since his mail order suit hadn't arrived yet. He would just borrow his pappy's Sunday suit. That would be no problem. Edna's wedding dress, ordered from Sears, had already arrived at the Russell house, and that was the main thing. Hopefully, nothing would stop them this time.

It had been so long since that Christmas more than a year ago when they first planned to marry. Obstacles kept popping up. First, it had been her mother's illness. Then when they went to Preacher Oakley to perform the ceremony, they learned that Edna, at age 18, was under age in the state of Kentucky and would need her parents' consent. Papa refused to sign the papers. Alvie even went through the ritual of asking Mr. Brown for his daughter's hand in marriage, which was the proper protocol for a young man in those days.

The answer had been a blustery "No!" What could they be thinking? Edna was needed at home. "Absolutely, positively, no" was his final word.

In spite of her papa's stubbornness, they felt they had waited long enough. There had even been a little house moved to the corner lot next to Alvie's parents' home in Poole that stood waiting. She was only 18, but he was 25, and they were both eager to start their own home and family.

As soon as Alvie left to drive the 2 1/2 miles back to Poole to begin his wait, Edna went into the kitchen to get supper. She first stopped at her mother's bed to see if she needed anything. Sarah Ann Duckworth Brown was a pretty little woman, only 35, and already ill and worn out from the births of seven children. She was willing for her daughter to marry and knew she would, but didn't know when. She herself had been a bride

Lawrence Brown holding Edna.
Sarah Ann Duckworth Brown holding Dalphon.

at age 16. It was common in those days for a girl to marry young.

From her parents' bedroom, Edna stepped directly into the large kitchen. There was a fireplace in the center of the back wall. One of the boys had already built up the fire in the cook stove in the corner. All she had to do was heat the food left from a big Sunday dinner and bake a fresh skillet of cornbread in the oven. The dinner was still on a large table in the center of the floor. Each bowl had been carefully covered with plates. A clean white flour sack cloth covered the entire table. The kitchen was also furnished with a cabinet and pie safe. A table near the door held the wash pans and water bucket. In the corner to the left stood another double bed where three of the boys slept. A bed in the kitchen was a familiar sight in homes with large families.

Edna took a pitcher to the smaller of the two back porches and filled it with cold milk from a crock. This was the morning milking. Milk from the evening milking would be too warm. It had been strained and left sitting for the thick cream to rise.

With everything ready, she called them all in to eat. Papa sat at the head of the table. Lawrence Brown was a tall, dark, handsome man, who kept his family well fed. He was a good man, but a stern father whose children dared not disobey.

Edna glanced toward her father. Her heart raced as she remembered that tonight would be her first act of defiance, and she wouldn't allow herself to think of the consequences if she should be discovered slipping out of the house later that night. Just like the battle of wills between the seasons going on outside, there was a battle of wills between father and daughter inside the farmhouse. The young girl couldn't help thinking back over the years and feeling a little sadness at leaving the place where she had been born. This was the only home she had ever known. It had been in the Brown family for four generations.

Her great grandmother, Elizabeth Rountree Brown, had brought her 16-year-old son, Henry (Edna's grandfather), to Kentucky from North Carolina in 1869. Before the Civil War, the Brown family had a comfortable life with large land holdings, slaves, a small wagon and buggy factory and repair shop, a

Cabin on the Brown farm

water powered mill, and a government supported still. The War had changed all that. Henry Brown's grandfather, Joseph Brown (m. Elizabeth Tapp), died in 1862, and his father, John Lewis Brown (m. Elizabeth Rountree), died suddenly in 1863, when he was only 45 years old. Much of the family estate was lost between 1862 and 1865. The devastating effects of the Civil War (and earlier weather and market problems) caused many Piedmont region families to migrate west where land was cheaper.

Edna remembered the log cabin in the back yard. Her grandparents and great grandmother had lived there before half of it became the hen house after the new house where she was born was built. The other half of the cabin was moved downhill where it still stands. Her grandparents then built a nicer house up on the "big road" (Highway 41) and moved there to live with another son and his wife, Uncle Charles and Aunt Lou Brown. Nothing in these memories would change her mind. Nor would the faces of her brothers and sister as she looked around the table and tried to memorize their features, not knowing when she would be allowed to see them again. Across the table sat her brothers, Dalphon and Dallas, who were already teenagers and could take over some of her chores. Next came Delmer and L.D., sturdy, good natured boys, who were hard workers.

Next to her sat cute little sister Estelle, who at age six could already bake homemade biscuits. She was also good help at chasing after the toddler in the family, little towheaded Eugene.

Edna knew the change would be hard on them. She was willing to come back often to help out, if Papa would allow it. But Papa might ban her from ever coming home again. She was aware of the risk.

With supper over and the table cleared, Edna took down the two big dishpans from their nail behind the cook stove and set them on the table to wash dishes. She used a paring knife to shave tiny curls from a bar of homemade lye soap into the larger pan, and then poured hot water from the kettle into both pans. The kettle was always kept near boiling on the stove. Her mother's first stove was called a Darling. This was the brand

Dalphon, Dallas, Delmer, L.D., Eugene

name, but it must have seemed like a darling since it was so much nicer to cook on than cooking in the fireplace. When the house was first built, Edna's grandmother cooked in the brick fireplace in this big new kitchen.

Estelle and newest brother Buster, born 1927

With the dishes done and everything tidy, Edna blew out the coal oil lamp in the middle of the table. Farmers went to bed early. No farmer worth his salt would waste a penny's worth of coal oil (kerosene) unnecessarily. "Early to bed and early to rise makes a man healthy, wealthy, and wise" was a motto they lived by.

Three of the boys went to bed in the double bed in the kitchen corner. The other two slept in the room with their parents. Edna let down the bed in the parlor for Estelle and herself. Like many people in those days, they called this simply the front room.

Papa had banked the fires for the night, and with little light to see by, Edna packed two changes of clothes into a cardboard box. This was almost her entire wardrobe. She put the note she had written earlier into her pocket and climbed into bed fully clothed. The only sounds were the ticking clock on the mantle and an occasional sputtering from the flames in the fireplace, trying to escape their blanket of ashes.

Soon, the sound of Papa snoring came into the room. The clock had just struck nine. Only nine o'clock? It was going to be a long night.

Back in Poole, Alvie was sitting by the fire with his entire family. His parents, George Areli Russell and Sarah Ann Tomlingson Russell, knew of the elopement and approved. This was to be the first of their children to marry. Their three daughters, Lillie Jane, Lila Mae, and Minnie Veneda still lived at home.

Alvie had someone to talk with, and that helped the hours pass by, but it was still going to be a long evening for him too.

> These two young people are my parents, and they did finally manage to be married, but not without a few more obstacles. While they are waiting by the firelight, I will have time to tell you how this romance began, just as they told it to me, 66 years later....

Daddy said the first time he saw Mama; she was playing the piano at Shady Grove General Baptist Church in Poole, where he began to attend after they moved from their farm 4 1/2 miles east of Dixon. Daddy and his father had bought a house on three acres and a blacksmith shop at the smaller of the two crossroads in Poole. The shop was on the left and the house sat on the second lot to the right of a short dirt road that crossed the main dirt road. The longest road went farther north and south than anyone in Poole had likely ever traveled. It was the main route from Chicago to Florida. After it was paved it would be renamed from the Dixie Bee Line to Highway 41 (now 41A).

Daddy had taken a big step to get away from farming. He opened an auto repair shop in the old blacksmith shop. This was a brave undertaking, because the horse and buggy was still a popular mode of travel in that area. Country folks were slow to accept the automobile. They were either afraid it would blow up or just didn't have the money to buy one.

Daddy had decided a long time ago he didn't like farming. He said it seemed they hardly made much more than enough at harvest to feed the animals through the winter so they could plow again in the spring.

He once thought being a barber might be an easy way to make a living and ordered a pair of hair clippers. After doing a butcher job practicing on a few relatives' heads, he said, "No, that's not the way either."

One day he saw an ad in a magazine for a school in Kansas City that trained young men in auto mechanics. This sounded very interesting. After a long struggle to get the hundred dollar fee, he was on his way. He drove his father's old Model T Ford to the train in Sebree. A neighbor, Huron Wilkerson, went along to drive the car home. Daddy was the only one in the family who knew how to drive.

They got stuck in the mud on a steep hill going home and had to be pulled out by a neighbor. In Daddy's first letter from Kansas City he showed concern about this hill and asked if they got hung up on it. My grandmother's answer was "yes." Her letters also expressed concern for his clothing being the right type to wear in a big city. This was a trying time for her to have her only son so many muddy miles from home.

The crossroads by the blacksmith shop is where Mama turned east to go to the little country school. She and her younger brothers walked to Poole from the farm each day, a five-mile round trip. The road went uphill to Brother Oakley's house on the right, and then took a sharp right turn. Just past the preacher's garden sat the three-room school.

Daddy also saw Mama at his Aunt Birdie Melton's house when he went there to visit. His cousin Fannie and Mama were best friends and Mama visited there too. Sometimes when Daddy saw them walking down the road together past the shop, he would hop on his bicycle to ride in circles around them, acting as if he were drunk. "That crazy Alvie Russell," she would exclaim to her family, after returning home.

The romance began a year later at a church business meeting and wiener roast at Brother Oakley's house. The members had decided to divide into two teams and compete for getting new folks to come to church. Daddy began talking to Mama to get her on his team. Along came Coleman Oakley, the preacher's son and current contender for her affections, and gave Daddy a shove. Coleman felt that Mama was his date for the evening since he had walked her to the meeting from Inola Allen's house where she had spent the night.

Daddy, being the calm, slow-to-anger kind of person he is, didn't let it bother him. Then came another shove. Daddy stood his ground, undaunted. Finally there was a harder shove in his back that knocked him to the ground. He still refused to fight and continued to talk to Mama.

Having failed to break up this conversation, Coleman went away, cooked a hotdog, and offered it to Mama. But she was so disgusted with him by now because of his shabby behavior, she refused to eat it.

Daddy said to her, "Would you eat one if I cook it for you?" She said, "yes." This obviously was the first of many yeses. The next yes was when he asked if she would like to go for a drive in his 1918 Buick. Mama admits now that besides all his other charms, the car played a major role in her decision. The thought of spinning around the countryside to go visiting was a thrill for a young girl who seldom had a chance to leave the farm. She was still only 16, but he was 23.

"Agile" and "sprightly" are words that described Daddy, but words like "balky" and "sluggish" better described his car. He says he had to waste a few weekends working on it before he could take Mama for her promised drive.

Finally, the big day arrived and, with his three sisters in the car, he drove up the treelined lane into the Brown's large front yard. They were greeted by curious faces looking at them from everywhere, out windows, around corners, doorways, and trees.

Company coming was an exciting event for farm folks. It didn't happen often. After that day they went for many Sunday afternoon drives. Dating was much different than it is today. For one thing, it was called "goin a courtin." They didn't go to restaurants and movies. They mainly went to church meetings and revivals at night or to a relative's house for Sunday dinner. One place they went to often was Mama's Uncle Charlie Brown's house south of Poole. They always had a car full of young people, usually Daddy's sisters or Mama's brothers. Few people had cars, and when one did roll down the road it would have been a waste to have empty seats with so many people wishing they could go for a drive.

Gladys Brown, Ruby Brown Stinnet seated. Laura Watson Newton, Edna Brown, and Alvie Russell standing. A Sunday visit to Uncle Charlie Brown's house

Soon, Daddy began to court her seriously, and asked her to marry him. She said, "yes," again. He later gave her a beautiful, full carat, genuine ruby in a tall setting on a narrow gold band. This was stylish at the time for engagement rings, and just the ring she wanted. Her friend Ruby Newton had received one from Everett Allen (Mama's cousin).

The engagement took place in October and they set the wedding date for around Christmas. She would be seventeen on the 25th. I don't know how they were able to accomplish this with the car always full of people, and even when they were alone in the parlor, they might catch Papa peeking in the window.

But Christmas came and their plans were dashed to pieces. Her mother became ill. All the responsibility for keeping a large family clean and fed fell on her shoulders. She dutifully carried out the role of a good daughter. The months slipped by, but her mother was no better. Christmas came and went again. Now Mama was 18, but what could she do?

As winter dragged on, they decided to get married anyway, but learned they couldn't without her father's consent. Preacher Oakley told them 18 was the legal age in Tennessee. They immediately began to make plans to elope. Daddy brought a tape measure and Sears catalog over to Mama's house. Together they ordered a pretty blue crepe dress with lace and had it sent to Daddy's address. He also ordered a new suit of clothes. Meanwhile, Mama practiced turning the squeaky front door knob.

On Sunday, March 14, the day Fannie and Herman came to visit, they knew the time was right, so they planned to meet at the big oak tree that night.

The long wait is almost over. We will check in on Mama now. She is bending over the fireplace holding her wrist watch near the dying embers to catch a tiny glow of light. The clock was taking such a long time between strikes that she often checked her watch too, but the hands had hardly moved since the last time. She may have remembered a riddle she learned as a child about watches. "Round as a biscuit, busy as a bee, prettiest little thing you ever did see. What is it? Answer: a watch." Busy indeed! This watch must be napping.

Finally, the time to leave arrived. Mama slipped from the covers, fully dressed, and took her cardboard box from its hiding place. She put the opened note on the mantle shelf and quietly opened the door. She could see her parents' bed in the adjoining room. Out onto the squeaky porch she crept. It was cold outside. A light snow was blowing. She made it to the yard, but there were still a lot of dead leaves on the ground that made a crunchy sound with every step. She held her breath. She was so afraid Papa would hear her footsteps, or the dog would bark. There was another worry: maybe Daddy would get lost and not be at the tree to meet her.

She hurried to get behind the corncrib and out of sight of the house. It was a dark moonless night, but she felt safer after she climbed the first rail fence into the horse lot. Across the lot was another fence to climb, then she would be near the big tree.

Meanwhile, Daddy had his own problems. A light snow was falling, making it more difficult to see paths and landmarks. He walked in a circle in the unfamiliar fields. More than once he had seen headlights from cars on Highway 41 ahead of him.

Corn crib on Brown farm.

They should be behind him, so he would turn around and start again.

He was waiting at the tree when she arrived. Mama shoved the cardboard box into his hands and took off across the field like a little rabbit. Daddy had a hard time keeping up with her in his thick clothing. He was dressed to be out in the cold a long time. Over his pappy's heavy, blue Sunday suit, he had on an overcoat, and under the suit were his long-handled winter underwear. Once Mama stopped and, holding her flashlight near the ground, turned it on a second to search for puddles. "Turn that light off," he hissed. "But I don't want to step in a mud puddle and ruin my shoes," she protested in defense. "If Mr. Brown sees a light in the field, he will know something is wrong. He will find you gone and be at the shop waiting for us." Mama consented to continue in the dark. The fields were familiar to her after all those years of walking to school.

At the Russell's house, Daddy's sisters helped her change into her new wedding dress while he went down to the blacksmith shop to get the car.

The old grey weatherboard house stood under the long row of locust trees that were planted years ago by her grandfather from North Carolina. This property had been in the Brown family years ago, before the Russells moved to Poole.

It seemed strange to be making final preparations for the wedding, so strongly disapproved of by her papa, inside the very house where he was born.

After Mama donned her pretty blue dress, she looked at her reflection in the dresser mirror for a final approval. There was little left to do. She didn't wear makeup on her pretty round face, with large, dark brown eyes and a flawless complexion. Her thick, dark shiny hair was cut in the jaunty, stylish bob of the 20's. A quick touch-up with a comb and she was ready.

They climbed into the Baby Overland auto and headed south. Destination: Springfield, Tennessee.

Their plans were to drive to Earlington and catch a train there, but the car began to act up so they pulled into an all-night garage in Madisonville. A lone attendant was keeping a fire going in the stove in the back. Mama stood near the stove shivering. Was it from the cold or from thoughts of Papa? She was still afraid he would wake up, find her gone, and follow them.

They decided to leave the car there and catch a train from Madisonville, but they had to wait a long time.

In the meantime, back on the Brown farm, dawn was breaking. Papa heard the rooster crowing. Time to get up and wake Edna to cook breakfast. He went into her room and saw she was already up, then noticed the note on the mantle over the fireplace and read that she had left to get married.

I can't describe his reaction; I wasn't there. I can only imagine. I do know he went out to the auto house (garage), cranked up his old model T Ford, and took off in hot pursuit.

His first stop was at his sister's (Aunt Hattie Allen's) house about a mile down the road, where she lived in a big white house with her large family.

He glumly announced, "Well, I lost a member of my family last night." They were shocked to their shoes; they thought someone had died.

Next stop, the Russells' house - but, no, they didn't know where they went. Papa Brown told the Russells he was going to catch the runaways. My grandfather Russell's response was, "They didn't leave here to be caught."

Then on he went to Aunt Birdie Melton's house and called for Fannie and Herman, but they were just as surprised as everyone else. Mama and Daddy had deliberately told no one of their plans so all could truthfully say they didn't know. Poor Aunt Birdie; She had been cooking breakfast, and the interruption caused her to forget the skillet of bacon on the stove. It burned to a crisp.

Papa headed for Shawneetown, Illinois, the most popular place for quick weddings. At Henderson police station, sixteen miles north, he stopped and reported his runaway daughter. When the officer learned she was 18, he said, "Fellow, it is awfully cold out today. Why don't you just go on home and leave her alone?" and so he did, for now.

After what seemed like an eternity, the train arrived in Madisonville. Once on board they had to endure another eternity, because that puffing monster stopped at every cowpath. It pulled into the train station in Springfield a little before time for the court house to open.

Not knowing where the court house was located, and being in a strange city, the safe thing to do was hire a taxi. "Sure," the driver said, "take you right there," and he did. Just around the corner he deposited them at the court house steps and collected his 50 cents. Mama and Daddy were miffed. They could have walked. Fifty cents was a lot of money in 1926.

They bought their license for five dollars and found the Justice of the Peace and a witness (no waiting period then). Now, after all the other things they had to endure, came a very serious hitch. The Justice took one look at cute, petite Edna Brown, and couldn't believe she was eighteen.

Mama and Daddy, being the honest people they were, hadn't suspected that anyone would question their word. They had no proof. Women in those days didn't drive a car, so she had no identification.

Daddy said they would just go on to Nashville. After the Justice of the Peace and witness cross examined Mama about her age and couldn't trip her up, they went on with the short ceremony.

So about the time Papa Brown was at the police station near the Indiana border, Mama and Daddy were saying their "I do's" in Tennessee.

When the Justice of the Peace learned they had no place to stay, he took them to an upstairs room for rent. It turned out to be his own house. Then they went to get something to eat.

They arrived home in the early afternoon the following day. After Mama Russell had fed them, Daddy learned there was a job waiting for him. Their old Model T truck was broken down. It was used every day to make a run to Henderson to pick up all the supplies for both grocery stores and the restaurant. It had to be put into running shape immediately.

While he was on his way through town to where the truck was broken down, he saw Papa's buggy hitched in front of Sam Royster's Grocery where he had a small watch repair office. Mr. Brown saw him. UH OH! Mr. Brown immediately ran out, jumped in his buggy, and headed his horse south to the Russells' house. He called for Mama to come out. Angrily he said, "You think you've done something smart, don't you?"

"No," she calmly replied, "I just think I got married like normal people do."

"Well," Papa said, "now you can just let the rest of the world go by." This is the title of a piece of music Daddy had given Mama for her to learn to play for him on the piano. Thrusting the music into her hands he said, "I don't want you or Alvie to set foot on my land again." Then he left.

The next day he came back and threw a box over the fence into the yard. It contained everything he could find that belonged to Mama, even an old pair of shoes from their dump behind the smokehouse.

Everybody was pretty miserable. Mama cried. Mama Brown cried. The brothers and sister all missed her and she missed them.

Daddy and Papa Brown belonged to the same Lodge. Three of the members called on Papa Brown and tried to talk some sense into him. It did no good.

Two months passed and somehow Aunt Hattie's husband, Uncle Bloom Allen, managed to pierce his armor. He took him to Poole. First they went to the shop to see Daddy, then to the house to see Mama. Uncle Bloom did most of the talking. Papa Brown told them it was all right to come home again. Nothing more was ever said about it after that.

Mama Brown recovered from her illness and went on to have another son, Buster. About a month before he was born, Mama became pregnant with Marvin. So mother and daughter were both expecting at the same time. Mama raised five children in that little house which was added to twice: Marvin Winfred, Jimmie Lee, Dorothy Jean, Anna Lorene, and Linda Christine.

When the big new garage was built, Papa Brown moved his watch repair business to the garage office. He had a wire cage in the corner just large enough to hold his brown desk with all the little drawers and white knobs, plus the tall stool.

Mama and Papa Brown lived a long pleasant life on the farm. Papa Brown died in a nursing home November, 1969, at the age of 83. Mama Brown lived to be 96 years old and died in her sleep in the same house where she had raised her family.

When I was growing up, I was not aware of any friction between the families. I have warm memories of holiday dinners in that big kitchen with the brick fireplace. Both grandparents always made us feel welcome.

Mama, at age 85, still wears her ruby ring plus a gold band. Over the years Daddy would ask if she would like a regular set of diamonds. Her answer was always the same: "No, I want to wear my ruby."

Mama and Daddy back on the farm. She is wearing her wedding dress and “round as a biscuit” wrist watch. The auto house is in the background.

OUR LITTLE HOUSE IN THE GARDEN

All the children attending Mama's three room school in 1925, who are still living today, will remember the morning they saw a little house slowly creeping across fields and cow pastures behind the school. Recently I asked Uncle L.D., who still lives on the Brown farm, about that day. He said, "Yes, I saw them move the little house. It was just three rooms then, I believe. I saw it from the window of the old school house. They used a steam engine to pull it and rolled it on logs."

While Mama and Daddy were making plans to marry, he got a chance to buy a house for one hundred dollars. But it would need to be moved. It was located on land directly behind Shady Grove Church that was destined to become the newest section of the cemetery.

Daddy Russell (my grandfather) already owned three acres on the corner across from the blacksmith shop, and it had three lots that faced the road. He planned to give Daddy the corner lot.

In 1922, when Daddy first returned from Kansas City with his newly acquired mechanic skills, he rented the blacksmith shop from Jasper Denning for five dollars a month but stayed on the farm. He was just beginning a new business and knew he should take one step at a time.

At this time all the roads in Webster County were dirt. The road that ran past the shop was the main route from Chicago to Miami. It had originally been an Indian trail that lead to the Natchez Trace. Later it was called the 'Buttermilk road,' when pioneers began to settle in that area. Farm wives would place crocks filled with fresh buttermilk at the entrance to their lanes for the refreshment of hot, thirsty travelers. There were no McDonalds then, or any other eating places, except for widely scattered inns. Now the road was called the Dixie Bee Line.

In 1923, Daddy's business was thriving, so they bought the shop for three hundred dollars. That same day, Daddy Russell bought the three acres and a house, for nine hundred fifty dollars, from George Cottingham.

Veneda, Sarah Ann, Lila Mae. Russell's house in 1923. Lawrence Brown's birthplace in 1886.

Mama's grandfather, Henry Brown, came from North Carolina in 1869 when he was sixteen years old. He and her grandmother, Emily Jane Pool, had once lived there. It was Papa Brown's birthplace. Mama's grandfather built the blacksmith shop and planted the long row of locust trees.

Now it was time to move the house. Two men, Fred Melton and Lil Poole, agreed to do it for twenty-five dollars. This only covered the costs. It was a generous gesture towards a young fellow who was getting married.

They used a steam engine from Mr.Melton's sawmill and rolled the house on logs. By removing the log it rolled off of in the back and placing it in front of the house, they could travel at a snail's pace across the fields. They had to tear down fences and rebuild them. Finally, the little house was deposited in the middle of the corner lot. This square of land had been their garden and it still had earth ridges, from hoeing and plowing, running all the way across the lot.

Daddy's Uncle Reuben Todd laughingly called it "Alvie and Edna's little Garden of Egypt."

The chimney broke and fell through the ceiling during the move. They still didn't have furniture when they married, so they lived with Daddy's parents and sisters for two months while they fixed up the house.

Some evenings they would all sit in the shade of the locust trees to rest and talk. My grandparents told my parents about their first houses. For a while after their marriage, in 1900, they stayed with her parents Samuel and Elizabeth Tomlingson. (This was another family who suffered hardships handed down from the Civil War. Samuel was only six when he lost his father in 1862 after the battle of Perryville, Kentucky. Daniel Tomlingson, from Indiana, fought with a Northern Army to help save the Union and end slavery.) Then they moved into a log cabin on the Aldrich place, across from the Tomlingson farm. Daddy was born there in 1901. Next they moved to another log cabin on a road between the Wanamaker road and 41A. This cabin had not been lived in for years and was said to be haunted. My grandfather had bought the farm where the second cabin was, but he didn't think he could make a good living off this land and sold it. They soon moved back to the first cabin where Lillie Jane was born in 1903.

Next they moved to a box house, also called board and batten, on the same farm. The walls are constructed with a single layer of upright planks, with narrow strips nailed over the cracks on the outside. From here they moved to Highland Creek Bottoms where they had crop failures from flooding and moved back briefly to the box house on the Aldrich place. Finally, in 1911, they purchased and moved to the Frank Duncan farm, four miles east of Dixon.

The first night they lived in the haunted log cabin, Daddy Russell stepped outside for a quick visit to the privy and saw a grotesque figure standing in the tall weeds, at the edge of the woods, staring at the cabin. It had a large body and glowing, yellow eyes.

He called through the cabin door, "Annie, hand me my pistol!" "What do you want it for?" she called back. "Just hand me my pistol!" he said again. Still no response. After the third try, he went into the cabin, got it himself, and came back out. Holding the gun in front of him with both hands, he slowly walked towards this mysterious thing, keeping the gun leveled at its head. As he moved closer and closer, it never moved or made a sound, it just stood there, staring at the cabin. Finally, after a few anxious moments, he was close enough to see that the body of this apparition was only a large bush. The eyes were two rays of lamplight, shining through holes in the cabin wall where two small chunks had fallen out of the mud chinking between the logs. They were reflecting off two tall stalks of weeds. He called, "Annie, come here. I want you to see this thing." She came to the door, looked out, saw the thing, and fainted dead away. She was so shaken and weakened from the fright, she had to stay in bed for three days. Mama Russell was a sweet, hardworking little woman, a meticulous housekeeper, a good mother, and a fine neighbor, but she was never noted for her bravery.

Perhaps we should give her credit for the time they were living in Highland Bottoms when Daddy was five. She rescued him from a partly built house he was climbing on, after it was surrounded by flash flood waters. In spite of her fear of water, she lifted her skirt above her ankles and waded in. If there had been any men around, she would have been as worried about them seeing her ankles as she was worried about the water. In those days it was considered scandalous for women to expose an ankle.

Daddy Russell once told me that when he was a small boy, all the women wore full skirts that touched the floor. He wondered how they moved around. They seemed to float. He said he didn't know they had legs until he was nearly grown.

This haunted cabin also made strange noises. Every day at noon, while they were eating, it sounded as though someone threw a brick against the outside wall. They finally learned it was caused by large spikes that would expand during the heat of the day and cause the timbers of a lean-to room to pop away from the wall.

All these ghosts fell under close scrutiny. Daddy Russell was not a man to be fooled easily or scared, period.

Part of the time they lived in the Bottoms, they shared a tiny house with Mama Russell's sister, Francis, and her new

George Areli Russell and Sarah Ann Tomlingson Russell.

William Alvie Russell's birthplace - 1901. Drawn from his memory by a great grandson Rob DeGraffenreid

husband, Reuben Todd (Daddy Russell's cousin). They got into a tiff about something one day, causing Uncle Reuben and Aunt Frances to move their table and chairs out to the smokehouse and eat their meals in privacy. They soon patched things up and were friends for life.

Daddy has memories of living in the log cabin where he was born. He was crawling on the floor in a blue and white outfit. Mama Russell was in bed, Daddy Russell was washing clothes, and a man was visiting. He thinks it may have been when his first sister was born. He can never remember his mother being in bed in daytime except when there was a new baby.

He also remembers the top of the chimney falling over and the two men who came to repair it. It was one of the old mud and stick chimneys. One man told the other that if he added grass to the mud it would make it stronger.

Now back to getting the little house ready to move into. Daddy hired Tom Darr, a carpenter who lived in the northwest end of town. The little house was near the south end. Mr. Darr had to walk across town to work on it each day. It was probably a full half mile round trip.

Mama and Daddy waited for a cloudless day to take the old Model T truck to Henderson to shop for their furniture. On muddy days it was best to stay home. Rain could turn the dust to ankle-sucking mud. There were two or three places in town that had stepping stones across the road to aid people in crossing from one side to the other and still keep their shoes on.

Daddy took the eighty-six silver dollars he had been saving in a sock, put them in an empty tire chain sack from the garage, and took them to the bank to exchange for paper money.

They were "all dressed up" in their best clothes, with their pockets full of money, to begin the long, dusty trip to Henderson, sixteen miles to the north. This section can be zipped over in about twenty minutes today, but back in the 20's it was considered a long trip. There were many curves and pot holes. Daddy said the pot holes were terrible.

One day while riding his one-cylinder, Indian motor cycle (about 1923), he hit a hole and did a complete flip, landing on his head and right shoulder. He was knocked unconscious.

When he came to, he didn't know how long he had lain there. His head hurt and a lot of skin was missing from his shoulder and right arm. He was really angry. He jerked the bent handle bars back into position and in spite of the leaking fuel and fumes rising from the motor, he jumped back on and said, "I'm going to ride you home even if you blow up." He had a bad headache for three days. He probably had a concussion. He attached a side car and continued to ride his cycle a long time after that and finally sold it for forty dollars and a wide gold band ring he gave to his mother.

When they arrived in Henderson, they went to William Oglesby's furniture store and picked out three rooms of furniture. For the two bedrooms in front of the house, they bought a blue iron bed, a pink and white iron bed, two rockers, a library table, a chiffarobe, and two rugs - one wool, one straw. A chiffarobe is half dresser and half a tall compartment to hang clothes in, with a full length mirror on the door.

For the kitchen (the narrow room behind the bedroom on the left) they bought a coal oil (kerosene) range, a varnished oak kitchen cabinet, six cane bottom ladder back chairs, and a round oak table. The table was the only item that was second hand. It extended into a large oval table and was the one we all sat around in the kitchen for all our meals until the house was remodeled in 1946, when we got a dining room.

Then they chose a linoleum for the kitchen floor and wallpaper for the entire house. The total bill was one hundred fifty-two dollars. They settled their bill in full.

When they returned home with their treasures, the little shop was too small to park the loaded truck in. The Crowley Brothers, who were competitors, allowed them to park overnight in their big garage downtown, free of charge.

Mama liked living in town. She could walk to visit family and friends and they could visit her. Her mother, as a new bride, had the exact opposite situation. She moved from the little town of Herman Valley, where she had a happy social life, to the Brown farm in the middle of the woods. (This is the grandmother we called Mama Brown. She was a friendly, popular young girl in Herman Valley. She often played organ music for gatherings of her friends. Her advice to her daughters was "Learn to play the organ and piano and you will be welcome in anybody's parlor.") Before her children came along to keep her company, she would often take her chair and sewing, sit beside the barn near the lane, and view the Graysons' house on the next hill, more than half a mile away. They were her nearest neighbors.

Mama and Daddy bought a few pans and dishes, just enough to get by. No one had bridal showers in those days, but friends and relatives would sometimes bring a house-warming gift when they came for their first visit.

Mrs. Nannie Tapp, who lived across the road, gave her a quart jar of home-canned strawberries. Two other women each gave her a bowl. Mama Brown brought her some home-canned goods and six hens. Mama Russell also gave them six hens; now they would have plenty of eggs. Aunt Francis brought a settin' hen. This hen would be sitting on a nest of eggs for three weeks to hatch baby chickens. This meant that in a few weeks after that, they would be eating fried chicken. Sometime later, Papa Brown gave them two pigs. Mama kept them in a little pen near the orchard to "fatten them up." Later they made brief appearances in the kitchen in the form of platters of ham, bacon, and sausage.

Moving day was busy for Mama. She had beds to set up, windows to wash, and window shades and curtains to hang. There weren't many boxes to unpack. They didn't own much.

They ate dinner at Mama Russell's. That afternoon Daddy's sisters came over bringing salt and pepper shakers they had filled and other things that would go on the table, such as sugar, butter, mustard, etc.

Mama had a pretty new flowered oil cloth on the table. All women had these for daily use because they could be wiped clean with a dishcloth. Formica and most plastics hadn't been invented yet. Linen table cloths had to be washed on the board, starched, and ironed. They were saved for Sunday company.

Daddy worked that evening in the garage until it was too dark to see. Then he went to his new home to eat. Mama had supper on the stove and a bucket of water, kettle of hot water, and wash pan on a little table on the back porch, where he could get washed up, while she dished up the food to place on the table.

This was their first meal together alone. They sat down in their new cane bottom chairs and filled their plates with hot homemade biscuits, mashed potatoes, salmon patties, canned corn, and green peas. They would be eating a lot of canned food from the store until they had a garden and flock of chickens. They ate by kerosene lamplight, while sounds of bullfrogs, crickets, whippoorwills, and the warm spring air floated through the square window. This little window in the back wall of the tiny kitchen opened like a door. They had been a long time getting there, but they were just beginning a long journey together that would stretch far into the future.

In the days ahead, Mama kept busy with her garden, sewing, and housework. She washed by hand, on the board, in wash tubs, carrying buckets of water from the well. She made her own soap in a big, three legged, black, iron kettle in the back yard. This kettle was also used to heat wash water and boil the white clothes. She made her own clothes and canned many jars of food to store in the dirt cellar under the back porch.

It would be a few more years before electric power lines came to Webster County. This meant there was no refrigerator, washer, vacuum cleaner, toaster, mixer, iron, microwave, or any of the appliances that women today take for granted.

She did not consider her life a hardship. It was the only way of life she had ever known, as it was with others around her. Mama was a born homemaker and mother, as she had already shown by caring for a family of nine. She loved her work and received much joy and satisfaction from it. Women, in those days, were taught that their place was in the home.

Daddy enjoyed his work too. He liked automobiles. It was a challenge to find what was making that strange noise, or why the motor wouldn't start, then to repair it and get the car back on the road. This pleased the owners because the inner workings of these newfangled contraptions were a total mystery to most folks.

He and Daddy Russell were equal partners in the garage business. Daddy liked people, but he was a country boy fresh off the farm. It was a relief for him to have his father up front to deal with the public, while he worked in the back. After the office was built, it and the gas pumps out front became Daddy Russell's domain.

The little shop kept filling up with cars to overhaul. Daddy needed to expand. He bought an old tobacco warehouse for four hundred fifty dollars to tear down for the lumber. The ball teams had been playing basketball games there and they didn't want to give it up. The school board gave him five hundred fifty dollars for it and let him keep one-third of the building. This was enough lumber to build a very large garage, with enough left over to build a divided shed for his chickens and cow.

The garage always had a dirt floor and was hard to heat. There were only a large stove in the back to work near and another smaller one in the office. Years later, he said he wished he had built it half as big and twice as good.

Nineteen twenty-six was an eventful year for them. They were married, moved into their first house, and built the new garage. It was also the year that marked one hundred years since the first family of settlers arrived there in an ox cart in 1826. John Poole brought his family from Nelson County, Kentucky (originally from Virginia), to settle in this area and build a flour mill. He had bought a twenty-four hundred acre land grant from a Revolutionary War soldier for a good horse and gun. This good price was due to the fact the former soldier had heard of Indian troubles in Kentucky and was afraid to travel that far West.

Poole was still a part of Henderson County until 1860 when Webster county was carved out of it. The north edge of the town is still in present day Henderson County which includes the two hundred thousand acre Virginia grant given to Judge Richard Henderson, for whom the county was named, and his partners for their part in helping open Kentucky to settlers. They had hired Daniel Boone to build a road through the mountains to Boonesboro near the center of the state.

Although 1926 was a happy year for Mama and Daddy, they also had a serious setback. They had both looked forward to having children, but almost as soon as Mama learned she was going to have a baby, she lost it. To add to the disappointment, the doctor told her she would probably never be able to have children. It was a sad time for them, but Mama, exhibiting her spunky spirit, pulled herself to her full five feet and proclaimed, "Well! I guess I can have children if other women can." By Christmas of that same year, although she may not have known it yet, she was expecting again.

The little house that had been planted in the garden was destined to grow and produce abundantly. It would expand to nearly three times its original size, and five children were to bud, blossom, and grow there. They would slowly spread to different parts of the country like many vines from a single root.

Mama and Daddy near a locust tree in their front yard. A Model T sits in the shadow of the repair shop across the dirt road from Poole's mill.

MYSTERIES OF BIRTH, DEATH, AND ELECTRICITY

After I am born in this story, the events are viewed through the eyes of the little girl I was at the time.

The year 1927 was a quiet year for Mama and Daddy until August 26, when Mama had to take time out from her late summer canning to welcome their first baby to the little house in the garden: a healthy boy that they named Marvin Winfred. Others present who had anxiously awaited his arrival were Daddy, Mama Russell, Mrs. Nannie Tapp, and Dr. Roscoe Duncan.

This was a happy occasion for the Brown and Russell families. Not only was Marvin the firstborn, as his parents had both been in their families, he was the first grandchild on both sides and the first nephew for all those aunts and uncles. He was going to have plenty of visitors in the days ahead.

In the next few years, there were several important events. Although I may not have them in the correct sequence, the first was probably the graveling of the road between Henderson and Madisonville.

Legislation had been passed a few years earlier to improve all roads between county seats in Kentucky. This was a boost to the automobile industry. Folks would be more willing to own a car now that they wouldn't be as fearful of being caught out in the rain in it. Horses could pull a wagon or buggy through the mud to get home, but all a car could do was sit and spin its wheels. It was too risky to take a chance on not being able to get home by nightfall to feed the livestock and do the milking. Now, there would be a good road that could get one at least within walking distance of home.

My next story is a sad one. Mama's fifteen year old brother Dallas died. All the family had come down with the flu. The doctor was called to the house, but he had run out of medicine and had none to give them. Dallas stayed up the longest to care

Mama and Marvin

for the others. He later became the most ill and developed meningitis.

Mama went over to help all she could until she took the flu. People from town and their church came out to help. The last day Mama was there Dallas called her to his bedside in the parlor and told her of some money he had been saving for Christmas. He asked her to take it to buy a new tie that would match his Sunday suit. He knew he would need it for his funeral.

Later Mama heard how he had called them one by one, into his room, to say goodbye. He held onto Papa Brown's hand and begged him to take good care of his mother and his little baby brother, Buster, whom he loved so much.

He said, "I am going to heaven. I have already seen the place. I will be much better off there than the rest of you left down here."

They rolled his casket beside Mama Brown's bed so she could tell him goodbye. Daddy wrapped Mama in a blanket and carried her into the church for the funeral.

Dallas was buried in the newest section of the cemetery near his grandma and grandpa Brown's graves. This was the area behind Shady Grove Church, from where the little house was moved. This was one of the biggest heartbreaks of Mama's life. She still can't talk about him without tears. "He was one of the best of the bunch," she said. "He was always thinking of others and doing kind things for them."

One cold winter day, when Mama Brown came home from the hospital, where she had had some repair surgery performed, Dallas had her feather bed, blankets, and quilts spread on chairs in front of the fireplace, so she would have a warm bed to get into as soon as she arrived home.

I never knew anything about Dallas when I was growing up, except on Memorial Day, when I helped Mama place homemade sprays of flowers on the graves. We made these from ferns and flowers growing in our yard, and placed them on all the relatives graves that we could locate. She never knew exactly where Mama Brown's mother was buried, because Mama Brown had been so young at the time that she could only remember the general area. Mama would leave flowers on unmarked graves, on the hillside near the road.

Life has its ups and downs, and soon it would take an upward turn. Electricity found its way through the hills of Kentucky, all the way to Poole. Daddy had the house wired. Mama said she was rocking Marvin when the man came to put in the meter.

The entire town would be coming out of the dark ages. There would be light bulbs hanging from the center of ceilings. They could be turned on and off, simply by pulling a string or chain. The entire room would be flooded with light. No more huddling near a coal oil lamp to see. As people were able to afford them, new inventions could be bought to make their work easier.

Radios would bring far away places and people right into their own parlors or bedrooms. A few folks already had crystal sets that required a tall antenna on the house and earphones for the listener.

In 1927, Daddy built his own set from a book of instructions. He used an empty Quaker oat box, two boards, wire, a row of bolts, knob and spring, and crystal cat whisker. It was only supposed to have a range of twenty-five miles. But one night, after Daddy had been fixing it to get better reception, he picked up Pittsburgh, Pennsylvania, and Des Moines, Iowa. Neighbors say Daddy had the first radio in Poole.

Mama said he was patting his foot and waving his arms to music that she couldn't hear and it irritated her not to be able to hear it too. With the new radios, a whole room full of people could enjoy music, comedy programs, children's fifteen minute adventure stories after school and the fifteen minute daytime dramas that were the beginning of soap operas. Special broadcasts would bring neighbors who didn't own radios to gather in a huddle in front of the set to listen. Daddy still has our first electric radio-a table top Emerson.

He brought it home one day in 1936 and placed it on a tall lamp table by the west window of the front room. Then he plugged it in and turned it on.

It was a tall wooden box with a curve on top and medium brown finish. The middle knob had a tiny lighted window above it. Daddy adjusted the dials and produced voices and music.

Jimmie and I were amazed. How did those voices get into a wooden box? Where did the music come from? Where were those people? They were not anyone we knew in Poole.

Daddy told us the voices traveled through the air. This answer didn't satisfy us. I knew that if I stood on the front porch, and yelled to the top of my voice, people uptown would not be able to hear me.

Jimmie and I loved the radio, but we continued to puzzle and ponder over where those people were. Finally, Jimmie found a solution. "There are little, tiny people inside the box," he said.

I squeezed in between the window and lamp table to take a good look at the things inside. Nothing, even as small as an ant, was running around in there. Then I noticed the tubes. Maybe these are tiny, domed cities, I thought. Their world is normal for them, and we live in a world of giants. Then I thought if they should look out through their glass sky and see me, they would be frightened. So I got out from behind the table.

I know this sounds farfetched, but it is true. Remember I was only four years old. Even at that young age I wanted everything explained in detail. If the answers to my questions didn't satisfy me, I created theories of my own.

The washing machine, with its gasoline motor, wringer, and two rinse tubs, was a big step forward for women then. It would be a big step backwards today.

Clothes had to be lifted with a stick from the almost boiling wash water and pushed between the two rollers on the wringer to squeeze out the water. The clothes would then be dipped up and down in the rinse water. They were passed through the wringer again to another rinse tub and finally into the basket to carry out and hang on the long lines in the backyard. Each piece of clothing had to be shaken thoroughly before hanging because it had been mashed as flat as a pancake by the rollers.

Sometimes they used their fingers to help the garment start through the rollers. This could be very dangerous, because fingers and an entire arm might be pulled through to the armpit. The rollers would keep turning, removing flesh. This happened to Aunt Estelle when she was young. It also happened to Billy's brother Jack, who had the presence of mind to put the rollers into reverse and roll his arm back out.

Mama didn't get a refrigerator until I was three or four, because I remember the ice box and ice man. This ice box, a tall cabinet, had a lid on top that opened to reveal a metal compartment where large blocks of ice were kept. We had a square cardboard sign to place in the window with twenty-five, fifty, seventy-five, and one hundred pound numbers on red, blue, green, and yellow backgrounds. This was turned with the required amount on top. The ice man could tell, either by number or color, which size block of ice to bring to the house without having to go to the door first.

The ice needed to be replaced about three times a week, because the block would be chipped away with an ice pick for pieces to fill the drinking glasses. It would also melt to run down a pipe into a shallow pan on the floor underneath the icebox. If this was forgotten and not emptied often enough, we had big puddles to mop up. Our first refrigerator had four tall legs and what looked like a round, white wash tub on top. This housed the condenser and motor.

I remember how Mama Russell protested when Daddy surprised her with a new refrigerator. She had never been one to accept change easily. I happened to be in her kitchen when the delivery men came with this modern appliance that most women would have moved into the house themselves, just to have it. They gave her curious glances, as she paced around the kitchen, almost wringing her hands and exclaiming, "That can't be mine! I don't have any use for that thing. Where will I put it? What will I put in it? I don't have a thing to go in it."

They ignored her and placed the new refrigerator on the back porch next to the closet door under the stairs. A few weeks later, I saw her bent over looking inside the open refrigerator door, shuffling food around on the shelves, trying to find space for one more dish. It hadn't taken her long to discover how nice it was to have cold butter and milk, ice cubes, and homemade ice cream and to be able to keep leftovers. She no longer had to feed leftovers to the chickens if they weren't eaten the day they were cooked.

The coming of electricity was followed by another big change. Daddy Russell got a chance to buy more property. The house and lot that joined his three acres on the south side was for sale. It had a large fenced garden and fruit trees, hen house, smoke house, coal house, and stables. The house was complete, with a well near the kitchen door, an upstairs, a porch across the front, two large front rooms with a wide hall and beautiful dark walnut staircase, fireplaces and chimneys at each end of the house, a large sun porch, and an old woman.

Yes, you read this right. An elderly lady named Mary Stevens came with the house as part of the deal. She had formerly owned this house and had deeded it to preacher McCormick and his wife in exchange for caring for her the rest of her life. The preacher had accepted a church in St. Louis and would not be able to fulfill his obligations, so he made it a requirement for the new owners.

This was an ideal location for Mama and Daddy Russell and was a much nicer house. They agreed to the deal and paid fourteen hundred dollars for the entire property.

Mrs. Stevens was a pleasant, uncomplaining woman, who was never any trouble. Daddy Russell said he enjoyed talking to her. She only lived two or three more years.

The move into the big house made it possible to tear down the old house for lumber. It had never been painted. They used the lumber to build an office in the new garage and to add a fifteen foot extension onto the front of the little house for Mama and Daddy's growing family.

They built a large room in the right half that we always called the front room. A small bedroom and open porch were on the left. This took up much of the front yard. I always wondered why our house sat so close to the steep bank in front.

Jimmie was born March fourth, 1931, one day after Daddy's birthday. He was the first to be born in the new front room. Daddy and Mama Russell, Mrs. Delia Russell, and Dr. Duncan were all present at this happy event.

Now Mama had two little boys to keep her busy, but she hardly had time to catch her breath and turn around twice before I was on the way. In spite of this initial eagerness to be born, I became stubborn near the end. I lounged around taking in food and gaining weight for three weeks, while I made up my mind exactly which day I would make my grand entrance into this world. This accounts for my being a plump little thing weighing ten pounds when I was finally born on October seventh, 1932.

A Mrs. Miller had been chosen to be the midwife, and she grew so tired staying home waiting for Daddy to come for her that she went visiting. When Daddy finally went to pick her up he had to go to still another house to find her. I was born in the same room as Marvin, the bedroom on the left side of the original little house. Dr. Duncan was also in attendance. He had a bad heart and became ill the next day. He died not long afterward.

It must have seemed to Mama that babies were falling out of the sky, because when I was two and a half, she was expecting another one.

It was about this time that the road through Poole was paved, and would become Highway 41. I don't remember this event but Marvin does. He said he and Kenneth Russell, a cousin, were standing under Uncle Willie Bridwell's maple trees, watching the men spread concrete over the gravel road, when a bird fell out of a tree. It was stone dead. Now whenever a bird or baby chicken 'bit the dust' near a Russell child it always got a decent burial. I had a whole cemetery for baby chickens behind the smoke house. Each bird had a matchbox coffin, a mound covered with dandelions or whatever flowers were growing nearby, and a half brick for a headstone.

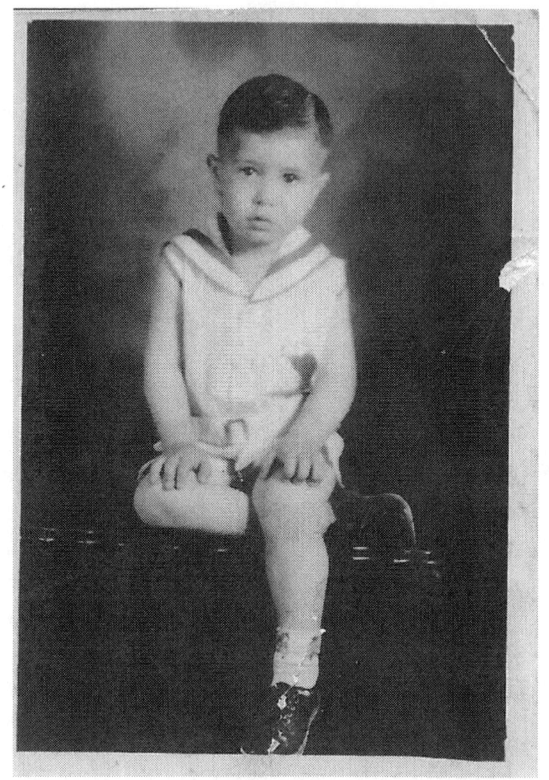

Jimmie

Marvin was immediately planning for a proper burial for his bird, when he was suddenly struck with a new idea. "I will give this bird the longest headstone a bird has ever had." He was thinking, "I will put him under the new concrete."

So, he climbed down the bank to the road and placed his little dead bird on the gravel just in front of the previous load of concrete. When the next load was dumped, the bird was entombed forever.

After this stretch of highway was completed, there would be hundreds of thousands of people passing over it, never to know they were driving on a six hundred mile long headstone for a little Kentucky robin.

Anna Lorene was born on a cold day in 1936. The exact date was February 7 (Laura Ingalls' birthday).

At this point in my stories it seems a light bulb comes on in my head, because I can remember this event and don't have to

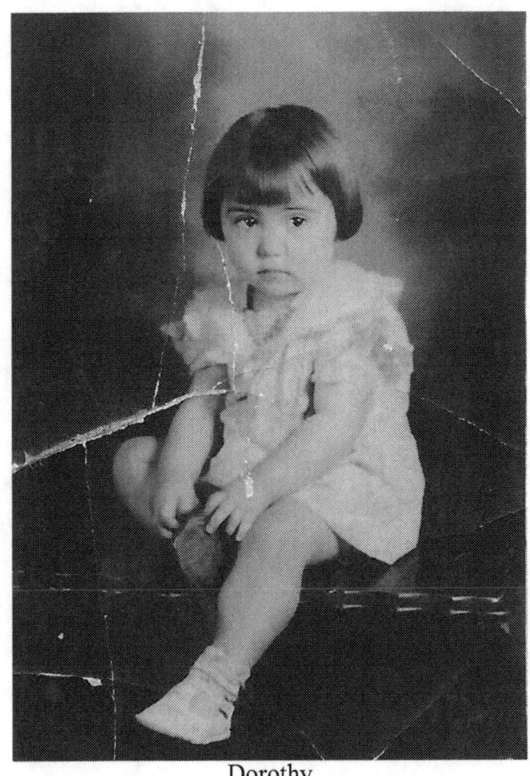

Dorothy

question my parents for every tiny detail.

I remember that several of us were ill. Jimmie and I had the chicken pox. Whatever was wrong with Mama was bad enough that Dr. Lynn, the new doctor in town, took her to the hospital in Henderson. When she was well enough to come home, they gave her a baby as a going home present, or so I was told.

Jimmie and I were taken to Mama Russell's house to stay a few days so we wouldn't give our pox to the new sister. I didn't know this was the reason I showed up in my grandmother's kitchen. I remember hearing my aunt say to the others. "Dorothy is here because she has chicken pox." This translated into my ears to sound like "chicken in the box." I looked all around the kitchen and bedroom floors, but I never found a box with a chicken in it. I was disappointed; I had planned to play with it.

Not long after this, my Aunt Estelle became ill and went to the hospital. She also received a baby for a going home present. Then I began to notice this same thing happened for other women.

One day a man came home from the hospital, but he hadn't been given a baby. "Why?" I wanted to know. But no one had an answer for me. This was the type of mystery that would send me off to sit on the pile of old boards behind the smoke house to think about.

While I was thinking, I came up with a new question. "Where did the hospital get these babies? When I asked the grownups to clear this up for me, they would tell me some silly story about a stork dropping them down the chimney, or finding them under a big cabbage leaf in the cabbage patch. Or even worse, some of them would suddenly develop a 'paralysis-of-the-tongue' condition and only be able to mumble.

Anna Lorene

One spring morning I made up my own story about the origin of babies. I was about six and Anna Lorene about three. We were standing in front of the hen house waiting for Mama. She was inside preparing nests of eggs for the hens that were ready to 'set' for three weeks to hatch eggs. She marked each egg with swirls of pencil marks, so she would only remove the fresh eggs each day. She shook each egg to see if any were rotten and would rattle. She threw one out the door and when it hit the ground and cracked open, a brilliant idea hit my mind.

I told Anna Lorene that three years ago Mama threw out a rotten egg and when it broke open there was a little baby inside and it was her. She didn't like this news one bit and began to cry. Then I was sorry and hurriedly told her it wasn't true. I don't think she has forgiven me to this day for that traumatic experience.

I believe my story was closer to the truth than the other fiction I had been hearing, now that I am looking back on it. Many forms of life come from eggs.

Linda was born October thirtieth, 1941, when I was nine years old and still had not solved this mystery. A family friend, Yvetta Young, had taken me to spend the night with her. I didn't think anything about it because she often took me visiting with her all over town.

She woke me early the next morning saying, "Hurry and get up and get ready for school. You have to have time to stop at home to see your big sister. Your Mother and Daddy got you a big sister last night." "Big sister," I said sleepily. "Where did they get her?" "Just get ready for school and don't ask so many questions," she scolded.

Me holding Linda. I loved my new sister even if I couldnt find out where they got her.

The Youngs lived at the north edge of Poole and I had plenty of time to think on the long walk home. "I already have a little sister," I was thinking. "It will be nice to have a big sister too. She can teach me things. They probably adopted her. She is probably twelve or fourteen."

When I entered our front room, Jimmie was already standing there in the middle of the floor, looking down into the big leather and wood rocker at the foot of Mama's bed. She hadn't even gotten up yet. "What is it?" he solemnly asked. "A girl" was the answer. "Shoot," he said, and walked on through the kitchen and out the back door to school.

I stood and looked down at this tiny bundle with its tiny face thinking, "Why this is only a baby, this is not a big sister." For a moment I was disappointed, then I quickly recovered and couldn't wait to get to school and tell all my friends. But I was disappointed again. I was too late; everyone already knew.

Later when I was asking around to find out where Dr. Lynn got her, they would only say, "From his little black bag."

One day Dr. Lynn made a house call because Marvin was in bed sick. This was a common thing for country doctors to do in those days. I decided while he was there I would find out once and for all where babies come from by going straight to the top man himself. Dr. Lynn would most certainly know where he got those babies.

Then came a hitch in my plans. I began to lose courage as I thought of this tall, stout man in his dark, three piece suit, with a watch chain hanging across his vest. He looked too distinguished and intimidating to approach. Today I think he looks like the doctor in the Norman Rockwell painting who is examining a little girl's doll with his stethoscope. I was about that little girl's age, but my problem was much bigger than a sick doll.

Suddenly, I was struck with a brilliant idea. I would tell Anna Lorene to do it. Yes, she was definitely the one for this secret mission. She had much more spunk than I did. She had already proven her courage that Christmas Eve when Santa made a live appearance at our house. Just the sight of him on the front porch, when Jimmie and I peeked through the long glass panes in the front door, sent both of us to the safety of the back bedroom.

We had to be coaxed back into the front room where Anna Lorene was cheerfully chatting with Santa and accepting gifts he was handing out from the heavily laden red wagon he had pulled through the front door.

Yes, Anna Lorene should be the one to get my answer from Dr. Lynn; she would be perfect. I pulled her to a corner in the kitchen and gave her the necessary instructions.

When Mama and the doctor came out of the bedroom Anna Lorene caught him just before he opened the front door and said, "I want to ask you a question." "O.K.," he said. "What is it?" "Where do you get babies?" she bravely asked. Poor Mama, standing there, was so embarrassed.

"I get them from under the Ohio River bridge and put them in my little black bag." he answered. "Well, do they have clothes on?" She also wanted to know. "No," he replied. "The people I give them to get clothes for them." Then he left.

I heard the door close and couldn't wait to come out of hiding. I had only heard muffled voices. "What did he say? What did he say?" I anxiously asked, when I finally got Anna Lorene to myself. She was beaming; she had the answer for me. When she told me they came from under the bridge, my heart sank to my shoes. I had gotten the run around again. I knew it was no truer than the stork and cabbage patch stories.

I sighed a long sigh and tried to console myself and accept the fact that I probably would never know where babies came from until I was a grown up and would then know everything.

When I was ten, and in the fifth grade, I still didn't know. I was every bit as frustrated as you are, reading this sad tale. Perhaps most children then didn't run into as many dead ends as I did. Never the less, in Kentucky in the 30's and 40's, we were still living in the Victorian age of morals and modesty. The facts of life were closely guarded secrets, discussed only by adults behind closed doors.

It amazes me that children today have all this information available as soon as they can talk.

One day at the end of history class, our teacher, Mrs. Gertie Russell asked, as she always did to finish a lesson, "Are there any questions?" On an impulse I had a new idea. Teachers know everything, I thought, and they like to answer questions, so I raised my hand. Dear, sweet, unsuspecting Mrs. Gertie said, "Yes Dorothy?" "Where do babies come from?" I suddenly blurted.

There! I had done it! I felt elated. I was finally going to know. But, I was running true to form: this didn't work out for me either. First there was a stunned silence that spread to the sixth grade side of the room. Then Mrs. Gertie was suddenly taken with the 'paralysis-of-the-tongue' affliction that left her only able to mumble. To add insult to injury, giggling and snickering began to fill the room. Soon, the bell rang to release us all from this quagmire.

I am sure I embarrassed Mrs. Gertie. This was a subject not discussed in public in those days. At least it was a question that had an answer. Back in the fourth grade, I asked Miss Emma Lou Fulcher, "Who made God?"

I went home from school that day as puzzled as ever, but I was soon to get a message as if it had been sent straight from heaven, where all life's secrets are kept. It was to be delivered to me by an older friend and schoolmate, Ann Long, at our next basketball game. During the game I went to the girls' rest room in the little basement under the stage. Ann followed me down the steps and stopped me in the middle of the floor.

"Is it really true that you don't know where babies come from?" she asked. "Yes," I answered. Then she proceeded with this fantastic tale that topped anything I had ever heard before, and that is why I believed it. No one could have made this one up; it had to be true.

That night in Poole High School, while the ball players were making small leaps to get the ball in the basket, I made a big leap towards growing up. I had the door opened to one of the most beautiful chapters on the subject of creation.

With that behind me, I can go on to discuss another beautiful creative force of nature that falls in a time period we call winter. This one could be observed right through the window panes of our little house in the garden.

Marvin, Jimmie, Dorothy, Anna Lorene, and Linda - 1945

WINTER AND BOUQUETS OF LACE

On the morning of the first big snowfall that I can remember, I had been awakened as usual by the sound of a roaring fire in the kitchen cookstove. It sat beside the door to our bedroom. These sounds and the light from the kitchen would rouse me from my long winter's nap.

Building up the three fires in the house was the first thing Daddy did in the cold, dark, early hours before daylight. I loved to lie in bed and hear the sounds coming from the kitchen where Mama was getting breakfast. After daybreak brought enough light into the bedroom, Daddy could see me stirring. He came in and lifted me from the daybed where I had slept since my new baby sister, Anna Lorene, had taken over my little iron bed with the tall sides. He said, "Dorothy there is something I want you to see outside." He carried me to the window and pulled back the long, narrow, green window shade. I blinked. The entire outside world was a dazzling white, extra bright because of my half-opened eyes. The yard was white, the big garage was white, the trees were white, even the sky was white with millions of tiny pieces of it falling silently to the ground. The snow was beautiful, but I didn't know what was causing it. I felt safe in Daddy's arms, and he seemed to be happy this was happening, so I was happy too.

"What do you think of that?" he asked. But I didn't know what to think. Besides, I was hungry and wanted to go into the kitchen where I could smell smoked country ham frying.

Mama was at the kitchen table rolling out her biscuits with her long-necked, blue glass bottle rolling pin. I loved to watch her do this.

The dough would stretch and stretch until it was just the right thickness, then she dipped the rim of a glass into the flour and cut rows of round circles until she had used all the places that were large enough for a biscuit. She dipped these one by one into a pan with a small amount of melted lard and turned them upside down so they would be coated on both sides. She gathered the star-shaped leftover dough and rolled it out again. I usually snatched a chunk to eat and another chunk to roll under my hands into a long snake. Mama would push her biscuits aside just enough to make room for the snake that I would bend into a wavy shape to resemble a crawling snake. After the biscuits came from the oven I had a hot, brown, crispy snake biscuit to go with my ham and eggs and oats.

After breakfast, Marvin and Jimmie got their wraps on to go to school. I wished I could go to school too but I was only three and would have to wait awhile. I couldn't wait to have galoshes and a cap with ear flaps and goggles just like my big brothers had. After they were gone and Daddy had gone to the garage to work on cars, Mama and I were left alone to take care of the baby and wash dishes.

I liked staying inside in the cozy house in winter. I had plenty to do. I could play with my paper dolls, or color, or rock my little woman rag doll in her Quaker oat box cradle. Mama Brown had made them for me during summers when I stayed a week with her while Mama and Daddy went with other members of the church to Oakland City for bible study courses.

Mama Brown made the doll with a large and a small square of an old sheet. After making little rolls she sewed them into a cross to make the doll. Then with embroidery thread, she made blue eyes, a pink nose, and red lips. An old fashioned bonnet, sewn on her head, covered the hair she didn't have, and a dress, with long gathered skirt, covered the feet she didn't have. For the cradle she took both ends off the oat box, cut a big slice off the side, and put the ends back on. Now with some folded cloth for a mattress and another square or pretty handkerchief for a bedspread, my toys were complete.

At times I had my grandmother's empty fireplace to use for a doll house. In the spring, when a fire was no longer needed, tidy, clean housewives would remove the grate and wash the bricks that lined the fireplace. They would then paste flowered wallpaper scraps inside. The hooks, that held the grate in place, poked through the paper and made perfect hangers for my doll's nightgown and Sunday 'go to meetin' dress when my little old woman wasn't wearing them.

Every winter, when I became old enough, I always made a new cardboard box doll house. I cut holes for windows and a door that opened. I pasted narrow strips of cardboard and cellophane over the windows to make window panes.

Then I would get an old Sears catalog out of the sideroom, where junk was stored, and cut out rugs, curtains, and people for my house. Sometimes I made cardboard furniture and would get dress scraps from Mama's big box to use for bedspreads and table cloths. She usually got this out in the afternoon, when all her other work was done, and work on her quilt tops.

Mama made many beautiful quilts of different patterns. She taught me to sew four little squares together into a larger square for a four-patch quilt. Sewing in front of the fireplace, with snow falling outside, was a pleasant way to spend a winter afternoon.

When Mama had a top finished, she "set up" her quilting frames in the front room. These were four long, narrow, strips of wood that she clamped tightly at the corners to just the right size. Then she set one of her cane bottom chairs under each corner. Next, she took the quilt lining and fastened it to the rows of small nails with sharp ends up. After this was secured and stretched tight, she unrolled a thin layer of cotton to cover the entire lining. On top of this she placed the quilt top and basted all the edges together. Now it was ready to quilt. Often relatives or friends came to help. First they would choose the design to be quilted. If the quilt top was elaborate they might follow the design exactly, or if it was a plainer one, the most common quilting design used was the "shell." Mama would take a pencil and string and lightly mark half circles about an inch apart, each one larger than the other, until they came to rest on the biggest circle of the last shell. This was an easy pattern to work.

I didn't know how to push the needle to make such tiny stitches. So I sat on the floor underneath the quilt and watched their left hands push the needle up and down so fast, I didn't know how they did it. I listened to their conversations but found nothing very interesting to advance my education. Marvin had better luck at the mill. He used to slip under the tall mill porch, which was used as a loading dock, and listen to the men's conversations. He fished in the millpond often and would see the men sitting on the porch in their chairs and be curious about their talks. One day he saw them standing in a circle with sour expressions; he knew something bad had happened. Maybe someone had died or a house had burned. He slipped back across the creek on the long board and quietly slithered around the corner and under the porch to see if he could learn what had happened. He heard one man say, "It's really bad. The bank is busted."

Marvin imagined coins spilling out. He had seen pictures of treasure chests tipped over with coins flowing over the top, so he wondered what a busted two story brick building looked like. He ran uptown to the half block of business buildings. The bank was in the middle of a row of five buildings on the west side of the road. He carefully examined the front of the bank and finding no signs of damage, he ran around to the back and gave that side a good inspection. Still no signs of being busted.

He was thoroughly puzzled by now and decided to go to the garage and ask Daddy. He knew Daddy could answer most questions. He even answered questions for the grown-ups. Inside the garage he said, "Dad, I overheard the men over at the mill say the bank was busted. I went uptown to see and there is not a single crack in it anywhere."

If Daddy didn't laugh out loud, I'll bet his insides were grinning. He carefully explained that busted was a word that meant broke, burst, or bankrupt, and in this case it meant that President Roosevelt had frozen the assets of the banks. This didn't mean the money had been put on ice, it meant no one could draw out his money now, and maybe never, because the country was in a depression. Later, people recovered their money from the Poole Deposit Bank.

Marvin got his first lesson on economics that day. He sometimes learned more in a few minutes under the mill porch than he did in a whole day at school. I have a pretty good idea

The old Poole Deposit bank building in 1989. Still no signs of being "busted".

that he learned more under the porch boards than I did under the quilting frames.

Getting back to the snow, when Marvin and Jimmie came home from school, Mama bundled me up in my coat and mittens, long cotton stockings, and a heavy scarf and let me go out in the yard to play.

The whole world outside looked like a fairyland. It was breathtakingly beautiful. There was a big, cold, mysterious silence to the air. The snow seemed to muffle all sounds except the sound of the snow itself, as it crunched beneath our feet.

To this very day I like to put on my boots and walk in circles in my back yard for no other reason than to hear the snow crunch. For a few unguarded moments I allow the suppressed child inside me to come forth, and I am six again.

A white icy coating of snow covered every branch down to the smallest bushes that were bent to the ground with their heavy layers of white fluff. The tall locusts and oaks and maples that lined the road had been magically transformed into giant bouquets of lace. We went down to look at the millpond. It was a smooth white circle like the top of one of Mama's iced cakes. Everything looked as if someone had taken a flour sifter and sprinkled powdered diamonds all around to glitter in the sunlight. We climbed the tree roots at the corner of our hill, and went around the house to the back yard. The only way up the hill was to take one of three paths. We didn't have concrete steps from the porch to the sidewalk in front until I was fourteen. The original wooden steps were torn out by Halloween pranksters.

Marvin and Jimmie built forts of large rolled snowballs to hide behind so they could pelt each other with small flying snow balls. I quickly learned to play on the other side of the house. Some of those balls came very near me. Later, when I got brave enough to go back, they were busy filling a big dishpan with snow. Mama handed the pan out the door and told them, if they filled it, she would make snow cream.

When they went into the house, I followed without even having to be told. We deposited our outer clothing on chairs in the porch or wherever they happened to fall. Then we hurried into the warm kitchen, where Mama was standing at the big oval table stirring milk, cream, and sugar in a big crock. She usually added black walnut flavoring.

We gathered around the table and watched as she stirred in the snow a little at a time, stirring it round and round with her big wooden spoon until the cream was stiff and could hold no more. After she dished it into five bowls, we ate and ate and refilled our bowls with this delicious treat until our mouths were almost frozen or we got a headache.

Daddy said, "When you get a headache you have had enough." He would get cold all over and go into the front room and climb on top of the Warm Morning heater to sit cross legged, Indian fashion, while he finished off his last bowl.

This heater had a metal jacket around it, with a grill on top to dress it up to be in a parlor or front room. The fire was in a heavy stove inside. He could not have sat on the inside stove that held the fire.

We would always laugh at him sitting there, he looked so funny. But then, we were never surprised at anything he might do. He often stood on his head or played magic tricks for us. He was a wonderful father, always doing things to make us happy.

We children always knew we were the most important part of our parent's lives. I can remember Daddy talking to total strangers, usually at church or in the garage, and bragging about how wealthy he was.

"I am a rich man," he would say. "Each one of my children is worth one million dollars, and I have five of them, so that makes me a multimillionaire." They would laugh at his wit and agree.

From our south window in the front room, I had a ring side seat to a lot of action in the winter. There was an uphill curve in the road between our house and Mama Russell's that was nearly impossible to drive over on ice. The pavement sloped and gravity didn't discriminate. It took anyone who tried to drive up that hill right to the ditch - local people, cross-country travelers, shiny Cadillacs, or 'beat up' Model A's. It didn't matter. They all came to a tire-spinning stand still.

Helpful folks came from everywhere to push and strain, put on chains, or put something under the tires for traction. These struggling, freezing people got no sympathy from the little girl in the window. She was having too much fun watching this live, action-filled performance on an ice-covered outdoor stage.

When I was finally old enough to go to school, I loved walking there in the snow. I had galoshes now. Mama and Daddy couldn't afford to buy them for me before. They couldn't waste money on something I would seldom use and soon outgrow.

Galoshes were like short, wide, soft boots that had a double fold in front that was fastened shut with a long row of metal clasps up the entire front. It took forever to get them all fastened.

I can never remember school being closed because of snow. I do remember that there might be only three or four pupils in my room. The buses might not be able to run, but school was open for all children who could get there. The children in town would be there even if we had to push our way through a foot or more of snow. The largest child would go first and make a path for the smaller ones to follow.

I loved the snow; it was never deep enough for me. I wished we would get a blizzard and snow drifts so deep we would have to dig tunnels to the chicken house and stables. I had read stories like this in books at school and envied the people who lived where this could happen.

I am sure my mother never had any frivolous notions like this when she was a girl. She had to stay on the farm enough without being snowed in to boot. She also had had a very frightening experience walking home from school one cold day in the middle of winter.

On this day she only had her brother, Dallas, with her, and she decided to take a different route walking home. She had been wanting for some time to go this direction so she could walk farther with some of her friends. Instead of turning south at the crossroads and following 41 to their road as she had always done, she continued on across the main road and stayed on the one that ran beside the mill and headed west. They walked out that way with the other children as far as Doris Allen's house, then turned south to continue across fields for a good mile to the Brown farm.

There had already been a light snow falling, and the farther they went the heavier it came down. The clouds and sky were growing darker, and Mama was beginning to wish she hadn't come this way. But if she turned around now, she would lose a lot of time getting back to the crossroads and then there would still be two and a half miles around by the other road. That would make them very late getting home, and she knew Mama and Papa would be worried.

As the snow whirled around, getting so thick they could only see a few feet ahead, they clutched their arms full of school books and walked close together. Mama grew colder and she began to have thoughts of stories she had heard of people being lost in blizzards and walking in circles until they froze to death. She could not be sure of her direction, since she could not see far enough around her. Mama began to get very worried now. She had always felt responsible for getting her younger brothers safely to school and back. She blamed herself for getting them

Uncle L.D. with ol' Ring, Circa 1944. In background are fields where Mama and Dallas were caught in snowstorm. Far left is the old cabin.

into this dangerous situation, because it had been her decision to go this way.

All she could do now was to put one foot in front of the other and pray that she was still going straight south. Houses were very far apart in this neck of the woods. At times the snow was so thick they could hardly see their own feet. Suddenly they bumped into something. It was a fence, and next to the fence was a big old walnut tree she recognized. What a relief. They were nearly home. This was the back side of their garden. Now all they had to do was climb over the fence and follow a ridge row to the gate. Walking through the garden gate put them in the back yard only a few feet from the back porch. Now Mama could see the soft glow of lamplight shining from the kitchen window. What a beautiful sight!

Never, never in all her life had Mama been so glad to be home. Never in her life had she been so glad to see anything as she was that big old walnut tree behind their garden.

No, I don't think Mama enjoyed snow as much as I did, but she would admit it was pretty.

Snow days at school were like a holiday. We got more attention from the teacher. She read or told us more stories, and we could play longer at the table where the clay and crayons and puzzles were.

After I was in higher grades, we could sit around the radiators to talk and watch our mittens and scarfs steam that we had placed there to dry. Sometimes those big radiators would go haywire and hiss or make a loud noise. The hissing sound would make us think they were about to explode and would send us scattering in all directions. Someone would run to get Woodrow Allen, our janitor, to rescue us from this impending peril.

Woodrow was a descendant of John Poole, the founder of Poole. He was a well-known man around town who worked at the school all the years I was there. In summer he was caretaker for the cemetery. Anyone who has ever gone to Poole school will remember Woodrow and his tool-filled coveralls, his cheerful smile, and his friendly disposition. He made friends with everyone.

I loved to come home from school on a cold day in winter and smell Mama's fried apple pies as soon as I opened the door. She would be at the big cook stove watching over a skillet full of these little half moon shaped pies while a big plate full already sat on the table cooling. She made these from apples she had dried herself and stored in glass jars.

Round circles of biscuit dough were filled with the cooked apples, seasoned with sugar and cinnamon, then folded and pressed shut with a fork to be fried in lard until crunchy brown.

The lard was made at hog butchering time by cooking inch square pieces of fat in a kettle. Here they simmered until they were transformed into a clear liquid and little crispy pieces that were similar to the pork rinds we buy today at the store. The liquid grease was poured into five gallon cans and would look like white vegetable shortening when cooled.

One of the nice things about winter was all the good smells that came from the kitchen: ginger bread, pumpkin pies, and popcorn balls to name a few. We popped corn in a long-handled wire popper in the fireplace, or Mama would pop it in a heavy iron skillet on the stove. She shook it back and forth over the smooth stove top until the lid lifted. The skillet would be overflowing with the fluffy white kernels.

One morning when I was very young I called Mama to come to the window and see the icy designs on the glass panes. We didn't have storm windows and with the heat concentrated in the center of the house, the outside walls grew very cold and thick layers of frost would form on the windows.

"Jack Frost was here last night," she said. "Who is Jack Frost?" I wanted to know. "He is a little man, with pointed shoes and a pointed hat. He carries a bucket of snow and paints pictures on the windows with his little brush, while we are sleeping," she explained.

I got my nose closer to the icy designs and studied them carefully. They were so beautiful, it must have taken countless little strokes to make all those pictures. I wondered how he did it.

Then I remembered the story Daddy told me about the poor shoemaker and the elves who came at night and sewed his shoes that he had cut from leather earlier that day. I also remembered the story of the elf who lived in the coal cellar and would come out only at night to sweep the kitchen and wash dishes. This Jack Frost must be their brother, I thought.

On long winter evenings Daddy told me a lot of interesting stories. I always liked the one about the wealthy baker who put loaves of bread in a basket for the poor children. He noticed one little girl who always stood back until the others had greedily grabbed the largest loaves and left her only the smallest loaf.

One day the baker put gold coins in the smallest loaf and of course it was left for the little girl. She returned the coins to the baker, because she thought they had gotten there by mistake. He said, "No mistake." He had put them there to reward her for her kind patience.

There was another story about how early man, who had always eaten raw meat, learned to cook his meat. A boy had been left at home to watch the pigs that lived under his family's hut. The hut burned, and when the boy tried to rescue the pigs he burned his hands on the hot flesh and stuck them in his mouth to cool. He discovered how much better roast pig tasted than raw pig. He told the others, and they tasted the meat. After that, everyone began burning down their houses so they could have roast pig.

I wondered as a child where Daddy had heard all these great stories, and I discovered his source recently when I sorted through some boxes from their attic on the farm. I found his old school books in a box and began to read the delightful stories in the McGuffy readers. And there they were. They had been shut up in those books that had lain unopened for 80 years. It was like finding buried treasure.

Winter snow and ice turned our town into a free amusement park. There were many hills to slide down on sleds and many frozen ponds to skate on. We could easily tell if the ice was thick enough to be safe, because there was always a hole chopped in the ice for the cows to drink from. We didn't have skates. We simply ran to pick up speed then held our feet still, one in front of the other, and slid on our shoe soles. We made snowmen, threw snowballs, shoveled snow, or anything to be able to stay out a little longer. Sometimes we would find a frozen puddle and have a smooth surface to draw pictures on with a stick.

Finally, we would get so cold and numb with raw legs and hands and noses that we were willing to go indoors to get warm. The house was a welcome, cozy place to be. We would get a washpan of warm water and soap and wash up for supper.

We could wash as often or as much as we wanted to in a pan of water, but a whole bath all over was for Saturday nights in the wash tub that was set in the bedroom in front of the fireplace. This kind of bathing was not pleasant in the winter. You could freeze on one side while burning on the other. We would have to keep turning, so our bodies didn't get too well done on the side next to the fire.

Two or three buckets of water had to be pumped and carried from the well. Half of the water was poured into the teakettle and large pans on top of the stove to heat. Then all this water had to be carried into the bedroom to fill the tub sitting on the floor. After the bath, it took two people to carry the heavy tub through the kitchen and back porch to empty near the back fence. The tub was then brought back in, cleaned, and placed in the bedroom again. The whole process had to be repeated for each person.

In large families of seven to ten people it is easy to see why this was not practical to do every night. This luxury was reserved for Saturday afternoon or night to be extra fresh for Saturday shopping and Sunday church and visiting. This was standard practice for clean people. There were some people who I think may never have had a good bath in their entire lives.

In ancient times no one bathed the way we do now. Even after it became a practice and soap was invented, it was still taboo in winter. It was widely believed that one would sicken and die if skin was exposed to the chill of winter air indoors.

There was a funny story about a local business man who went to a convention in a large city. He was inspecting the bathroom and admiring the large tub. "Sure would be a good place to take a bath if it was just Saturday night," he remarked to his roommate. We have always wondered why he couldn't have made an exception that one time. I remember a conversation I overheard while walking uptown one Saturday afternoon. A man stepped onto the sidewalk all spruced up in clean clothes and slicked down hair. A man walking ahead of me complimented him on his fresh appearance. The clean man jokingly said, "Yes, I take a bath every Saturday, whether I need it or not."

Wash day in winter was another difficult chore for women in those days. There were no clothes dryers. The laundry was always done on Monday. In large families it might take two days if done on a wash board. Ironing took one or two days. All this had to be completed by Thursday because cleaning house and cooking and bathing took the last half of the week. All work must be done before Sunday which was reserved for Church, a day of rest, and company.

Drying the clothes was the most difficult part. If a woman had an attic or basement to put clotheslines in she didn't have it so bad. But Mama had neither. She had nails in the top of the window and door facings in the front room. She tied a rope to the front window, then wove it back and forth across the room, hooking it over each nail until she had several lines for the wet laundry.

If we forgot and came in the front door, we would have to duck our heads and pick our way through sheets and other damp garments to find a path to the kitchen.

This was not a practice exclusive to the hills of Kentucky. It had to be done this way all over the world. Even First Lady Abigail Adams had to hang her family wash in the empty east room of the new White House, in the early 1800's.

Mama would hang her laundry outside in the winter if the sun was shining and there was the slightest chance it would dry. But the sun could be deceiving. The temperature might drop below freezing and the clothes would not have time to dry in the short daylight hours. Large heavy pieces like work pants and long handled underwear would be as stiff as a board.

We would bring them in like that and stand them against the wall. Anna Lorene and I, in our mischievous mirth, would laugh at those invisible people in their frozen clothing. We watched them take on comical postures as they slowly thawed and slumped to the floor to lie in wilted heaps.

Winter evenings were family time. No one went anywhere and we didn't have television. We had never even heard of it until after World War II, when Uncle Eugene, who was working in Chicago, came home one summer and told us about it.

After supper was over and the dishes were washed, we would all gather in the main bedroom and sit in front of the fireplace. We would talk or listen to programs on the radio, such as Lum and Abner, Amos and Andy, Jack Benny, Fibber McGee and Molly, or Lux Theater.

When the clock on the mantle said bedtime, I would change into my long flannel nightgown and crawl between the blankets on a feather bed. Mama made this bedding herself, with feathers she plucked from her mother's geese. She had tossed and plumped the bed to its full thickness with her hands. Sinking into it the first time was like falling into a cloud.

Sometimes Marvin sat on the edge of my bed and told me stories that he made up about animal families that lived in the woods. Sometimes Daddy tucked me in and pulled Mama's homemade quilts up to my ears. He would say, "Go to bed, sleep tight, get up in the morning and eat good oats." It didn't rhyme, but it sounded good. I loved oats swimming in cream and sugar. I think Daddy ate oats every morning of his life. I always thought this "eat good oats" saying came from his childhood. But he told me recently that my brother Jimmie is the one who started it.

I would lie in bed and watch Daddy knock the ashes out of the grate with the poker. Then he would dump a bucket of coal on top of the fire and shovel a thick layer of ashes on top of the shiny black lumps. This covering kept the fire from burning too fast during the night, so there would still be hot coals in the morning to start a roaring fire.

After the light was out, and I had said my little memorized prayer that began with, "Now I lay me down to sleep," there was nothing left to do but snuggle deeper into my warm, cozy, hollowed out place in the feathers and watch the flickering shadows on the ceiling and walls, made by the small patch of flames that always managed somehow to poke through the covering of ashes and crackle and sputter at the front edge of the grate.

I could hear the cold, howling wind outside. It made a low, lonely moaning sound as it whipped around the corners of the house. I felt safe with Mama and Daddy in their double bed in the corner opposite Anna Lorene's baby bed. My big brothers, Marvin and Jimmie, slept in the little room next to ours.

Darkness settled down, all around, to hug the town. The moon drifted overhead, high above the treetops, playing hide and seek with the clouds. This cozy atmosphere, on a cold winter's night, soon brought a peaceful sleep to all the occupants of our little house under the locust trees.

WINTER
IN SCHEESSELE'S WOODS
(a neighborhood treelot)

Walking alone in the snow at night,
I see it shimmering in the pale moonlight.
I am alone here
In the cold night air,
Yet I feel a warmth from this blanket of white.

The woods are a fairyland I alone have found.
There are tiny snowflakes tumbling around.
Is it a dream or is it real?
This ecstasy I feel,
As I see the white crystals float to the ground.

The snowy branches against the sky's deep face
Look like giant bouquets of fluffy frosted lace.
No, I'm not alone here,
In the cold night air.
The Spirit of Peace is in this mystical place.

Dorothy (Russell) DeGraffenreid
December, 1992

LIGHT, SLOW, NIGHT SNOW

What is more tranquil
Than a long winter night.
When the wind is so still
And gentle with white?

Who can explain
Why again and again,
Upon greeting this sight,
We find peaceful delight?

How crystals entwined
Inspire calmness of mind,
Touching hearts all around
Merely drifting earthbound,

Enchanting this eve
With encompassing hush,
Has never been learned
From our saddening rush.

What is more tranquil
Than a long, winter night.
When clouds with their chill
Still warm us with white?

I can explain
Snowflakes turning to rain
Or cooling and back
Into solid again.

But try as I might
On this lone winter night,
I know not wherefore,
This delicious respite.

Marvin Russell, February, 1979

THE LITTLE GREY CABIN BEHIND THE PINK ROSES

In the spring of 1937, when I was four and one half years old, I began to expand my boundaries. My world was no bigger than our yard and the view I had in all directions around it.

Our house, in the little town of Poole, Kentucky, stood on a low hill on the southeast corner of a cross roads where a narrow gravel road crossed Highway 41. My view to the North was blocked by Daddy's big garage where he worked on cars all day. All I could see beyond it were the tree tops lining the creek that ran along the far side of the long, low building.

Everything I could see looking west was across the highway. It might as well have been in a foreign country, because I was not allowed to go near the two lane strip of concrete that ran out of sight in both directions.

I didn't know where the road would take us, but Daddy once said if we got into our little blue car and drove north and kept going that same direction, never turning left or right even if we crossed mountains and oceans, we would eventually come back into town from the south side. This thought stretched my mind considerably because I couldn't understand how this could happen without coming back through Poole first.

Daddy explained that the earth is round. I had my first lesson about planets that day.

Straight across the highway from my front yard in this never never land where I could not venture was another tall bank covered in trees and honeysuckle vines. To the right was the big mill. To the left stood a big white Victorian house with gingerbread trim and two front porches, one on each side of a room that stood out in front. It was a pretty house with a long front lawn. Mr. Burr Tapp, one of the men who worked at the mill, and his wife, Mrs. "Nanny" Thornberry Tapp, lived there. In the cool evenings I could hear him pushing his clanking lawn mower back and forth over the grass. It was a nicer sound than the power mowers we have today.

The little crossroads. Background - Russell's garage, Baker's cabin, our house. Foreground - granary, Tapp's barn.

Looking south from my yard, I could see my grandparents' big white house with a porch all the way across the front. It had a porch swing, a common luxury in those days. Every evening, when my grandfather quit work and locked his office and the gas pumps in the front of the big garage, he walked past our house along the sidewalk at the foot of our hill and headed straight for his swing. He would sit lengthwise across the swing with his feet stretched out on the seat and swing sideways. I could hear the squeak, squeak of the chains even though there were two empty lots between our houses. This was too far away for me to go alone, but I had been down the narrow dirt path to their lane that led to the stables to watch Daddy or my biggest brother Marvin milk the cow we shared with them.

My grandparents took the milk from the morning milking and we took the milk in the evening because the cow gave a bigger bucketful then and we had more children in our family to drink it. Later we each had our own cow.

I had been taken for visits to my grandmother's house a few times, especially on Christmas Eve. A little more than a year earlier my brother Jimmie and I spent a few days and nights there when we had chicken pox. Mother had been to the hospital and when she came home, the nurses had given her a new baby girl for a going home present. We had to stay away from her until we were well.

From the backyard looking east toward where the sun came up every morning, I could see a white farmhouse on a hill. Brother Oakley, our Gèneral Baptist preacher, had once lived there, but now the Fulcher family occupied it. Mr. and Mrs. Fulcher had three grown daughters, Virginia, Albertine, and Emma Lou, who were to become my teachers in my first four grades.

Their house was too far away for me to visit alone. Our garden, chicken yard, and cow pasture lay in between. I never went in the cow pasture. I was afraid the cow might eat me, or I might fall into the pond and drown because I couldn't swim. Most little girls in those days didn't learn to swim because no one had swimming pools, and the nearest city pool was in Henderson, a long sixteen miles to the north. We went that far away only about three times a year, for Easter and Christmas shopping, and in the fall for new school shoes and supplies. Boys could go to the ponds and creeks to swim, but little girls had to stay at home with their mothers and learn to wash dishes and help take care of the babies.

The garden and chicken yard were the main places I could set my feet into outside the boundaries of the yard. For one thing that is where the outhouse was. We and our Poole neighbors

Burr and Nanny Tapp's house 1993

didn't have indoor plumbing until after World War II. I could go there to help Mama gather eggs and shell corn to feed to the chickens. As fast as the kernels came off the cob and landed in the dirt, the chickens gathered at our feet in a thick bunch, even climbing on top of each other in a frantic effort to pick the kernels off the ground with their pointed beaks.

That spring I was big enough to help in the garden. After Daddy had cleaned out the stables and spread the manure over the ground, he plowed it in with a farm tractor, then disked it to cut up the clods. After he smoothed it down with a heavy drag, the garden would be level with a fine rich soil and ready for the hand plow to cut little ditches all the way across. Mama taught me to drop the bean seeds three inches apart all the way down the row to the edge of the garden where a fence ran along the narrow gravel road.

I knew there was a little grey, weather beaten cabin across the road facing our garden. I could see it through the sweet pea and honeysuckle vines that grew along the fence. I knew that two very, very old people lived there, because I would sometimes see them sitting on their front porch. A board walk about eight feet long was all that separated the porch from the narrow road, so I had a close-up view. I knew they were old because their hair was grey like the old man who worked at the mill. I knew they were very, very old because their skin was so brown. I had seen how brown the farmers got from working in the fields when they passed by my house in horse-drawn wagons and on tractors. They had tans as brown as the nuts that fell from the trees. I knew it must have taken many summers, with tan on top of tan, for these people to become so brown.

My grandparents' house 1993

When I asked Mama about them, she told me they had lived there as long as she could remember. They were there when she was a little girl living on a farm two and a half miles southwest of town. She walked past their house every day on her way to the little school on the road beyond the Fulcher's house. Their names were James and Alice Baker, but everyone called the man by his nickname, "Heck."

After we finished working in the garden and had rows of corn, tomatoes, potatoes, squash, cucumbers, cabbage, peas, turnips, okra, and other things planted, we could rest and watch for it all to pop out of the ground and grow. It was fun to watch these long rows of little green plants get bigger and bigger. But there were times when I would be bored.

Marvin was five years older and could go off to play with his friends or go fishing with Heck. Jimmie and I couldn't stay around each other very long without getting into a fight. He didn't like for me to stick out my tongue at him, and I didn't know how to stop. I think I may have had the urge to do this because he wouldn't let me look at his comic books. He had a whole box full in his room. I would sometimes sneak one out to look at when I knew he was gone, then carefully slip it back into the exact place I took it from. He always knew somehow that I had been in his box and be mad at me. "Mama, Dorothy has been into my comic books again; now make her stay out," he would yell.

Jimmie also had a slingshot. He became such an expert that he could hit anything he aimed it at. Sometimes he pelted me with paper wads. This was another reason to stay out of his sight. He also kept his distance from his pesky sister, whom he didn't want near his personal things that he kept so neat and tidy.

Jimmie's desire for perfect order and neatness showed up at a very early age. One day when his slingshot broke, Uncle Eugene tied the two narrow strips of rubber inner-tube back together so he could fire it again. Jimmie didn't like the looks of this bulky knot. He took the scissors and trimmed it down. All too late, he realized what he had done, for it fell apart again.

With no brothers to play with very often, a little sister who couldn't talk, a mother who was often too busy to talk, and a

Jimmie riding our goat. Background is mill, Russell's garage, our garden, and Baker's cherry tree.

small world that I could look at but was not able to explore, I decided to escape.

One day during this spring of 1937 I sneaked down the path at the back corner of the yard and went in the back door of the garage to see Daddy and anybody else who might be in there. I only had to cross the gravel road that seldom had any traffic, then follow along the fence at the back of a lot that had a few cars and junk parked in it. This part of the fence that surrounded the little grey cabin was completely covered with a thick mass of beautiful pale pink roses. Only the chimney and peak of the cabin could be seen above it. At the back corner near the gate stood a board well. All of this together created a beautiful country scene. A car had stopped for gas at my grandfather's gas pumps in front of the garage, and a woman must have noticed how pretty it was too, because she walked back there with her camera and snapped a picture.

I went through the back door of the garage, passing near the well. My grandfather filled his bucket from this well and carried it through the garage to set on his desk in the office up front. There was a dipper in it for anyone to drink from. People in those days didn't think much about germs. They didn't pay much attention to things too small to see.

It was cool and shady inside the big building with a dirt floor. Large square posts held up the roof that sheltered cars and machinery inside. Through a square window in the roof I could look up and see the sky. There were a lot of interesting things to look at in there and nobody to stop me. Daddy was on the ground on his back under a car.

I soon found his grinding tool and a pile of metal shavings. I picked up a U-shaped magnet nearby and played with the shavings. There was some kind of magic in this piece of metal that would pull the shavings into designs. I would wipe them off and do it again.

Then I noticed the shiniest car I had ever seen. I walked over to it and could see my pretty print dress in it just as plain as I could in our chiffarobe mirror. Mama had made that dress for me on her treadle sewing machine.

Mr. Beckley Osbourne, a farmer who lived on a farm south of town, owned this car. It was a 1922 Model T Roadster. Only the passenger side had a door. He was so particular with it that he took it apart in the winter and wrapped the tires and other pieces to protect them. He then hung the body of the car from beams in his barn to keep it off the ground so it wouldn't rust. He was not about to drive his car on muddy roads in the winter and get it messy. He had asked Daddy if he thought he had done enough to protect his car and Daddy said, "I believe that ought to do it."

I have heard that a Ford company executive (around 1950) went to see Mr. Osbourne and tried to trade a new car for it and Beckley refused the offer. (This story has not been verified.)

Now it was spring and he had brought his beautiful car into the garage for a tuneup. He saw me standing too near that precious car and said, "Alvie, she is liable to get fingerprints on my car." He had a slow, cultured, distinguished way of talking that was different from other people. In many ways he was different from other people. One day he came to town with a load of Christmas gift socks he had collected over the years, took them to the grocery and traded them for bologna.

When he became upset that I was too near his car, Daddy told me gently, "Dorothy maybe you had better run on and find another place to play. You might get grease on your dress in here and then your mother would be upset."

Well, I expanded my world a little that morning, but it didn't do me much good because I couldn't touch it or let it touch me.

As I went out the back door and started home the way I had come, I saw the old woman at her well near the pink roses. She was struggling to pull up a bucket of water from deep down in the ground. The little wheel at the top of the wooden frame was squeaking with every turn.

She looked tired, so I stopped and asked her if I could help. She handed me the rope and it almost jerked me off my feet when she let go. "What was in that bucket anyway, a rock?" I managed to get it near the square hole of the big wooden box that had been built over the brick-lined hole to keep people and animals from falling into the deep water.

Alice took hold of the bucket and poured it into another bucket to carry into the house. Then she put the lid down over the hole and turned the well bucket upside down over the lid. I tried to help her carry the water into the cabin, but I think I mostly helped her splash little puddles on the long boards that she used for a sidewalk. Once inside, she lifted the bucket of fresh water onto a table to the right, just inside the back door. She dipped water into a wash pan on the table and washed her hands with a bar of lye soap, then dried them on a towel that was hanging on a nail on the wall at the end of the table.

"Direthy," she said, "would you like to watch me make biscuits?" Well, I thought, Alice knows my name except she didn't pronounce it right. I didn't want to correct her because I was afraid I might hurt her feelings. Mama had always told me never to hurt anyone's feelings. I knew, even if I had to walk a long way around feelings to avoid stepping on them and hurting someone, that I must do it. I never told her my name was Dorothy with two O's. She always called me Direthy.

I looked around the room. Straight ahead opposite the back door was a door into a larger room. This little kitchen was long and narrow. It looked as if someone had started to build a square room then ran out of lumber and cut it in half.

On each side of the door to the other room were two tall china cabinets. One had a shelf to use as a work top. There was a long window without curtains at the far end of the room to the left. A big cookstove, like the one Mama had, sat across the back corner. Although it was a warm spring day, there was a fire in it. A bucket of coal and a woodbox sat on the floor to my left. Coats and sweaters hung on nails on the wall above the woodbox.

A small square window with a view toward the highway was at the other end of the kitchen. Underneath was a large barrel that came almost to my eyes. Alice lifted the big dough board off the top and reached inside. I knew what was in there because my Grandmother Russell had one just like it in her kitchen. It was full of white flour from the mill across from Daddy's garage. That mill was the only skyscraper we had in Poole. It was a full three stories tall.

Farmers came from far out in the countryside to bring wagons and trucks loaded with wheat and corn to be ground into flour and meal. The engine puffed and chugged all day except for an hour at noon when it was shut down so the men who worked there could go home for dinner.

Alice filled her mixing bowl half full of flour, then added lard, soda, salt, and a cup of milk she had left near the stove to sour and clabber. It rolled out of the cup in big, thick chunks. This sounds awful, but it is the method pioneer women used to make their biscuits rise. Soda and sweet milk would not form the little bubbles in the dough that were needed to make it puff up. Then she put her hands into the mixture and worked it through her clean fingers just like I had seen Mama do, until she had a big soft ball. She dumped the ball onto the dough board that covered the barrel and rolled it flat with her longnecked, blue glass bottle rolling pin. When it was the right thickness, she dipped the rim of the glass in flour so it wouldn't stick to the dough and cut rows of circular shapes to put in a long flat pan. She placed this pan in the oven; then she lifted a circular metal piece out of the stove top with a handle that was made to fit and shoved in some more wood.

At that moment I heard the mill shut down. OH! OH! I knew I had better go home. It was dinner time and Mama would be looking for me. Alice went out the door with me and pointed to her little strawberry patch in the yard just behind the rose-covered fence. "Come back after you have had your dinner," she said, "and if you help me pick these berries, I will give you some to eat."

After dinner I told Mama I had to go help Alice pick strawberries and she was going to let me eat some. "Alright," Mama said, "but now don't you eat them all up from her. I don't imagine she has many in that little yard and she will need them to make a strawberry shortcake for her and Heck to eat."

I went down to the cabin. Alice brought out a half gallon sorghum molasses bucket, and we picked it nearly full. I only ate a handful because I knew we would be getting big buckets full from Uncle Tom. His patch was nearly as big as her whole yard.

After this day I became Alice's shadow. Everytime I saw her out, I would run down the road and go through her little front gate between the cherry trees. I was happy now, because my tiny world had grown a little larger and I had new places to explore.

Alice took me with her one day to pick wild greens that grew along the ditches. We went all the way up the hill to the Fulcher house, turned south at the sharp curve and went on down the road toward the cemetery. We passed a four room, white frame house on the right where Mama's little school used to be. Two rooms of the school had been saved and moved to the back of the lot to be used as stables. Cows lived there now, but they had no use for the blackboards still in it. These blackboards were simply sections of the board walls painted black.

We walked a little farther where the road narrowed into a lane and the gravel ended. Alice showed me a blackberry patch. "Later in the summer when the berries are ripe, I will bring you here and we can pick all the blackberries we want," she said.

Our bucket was full of greens by now - lambs quarter, wild lettuce, narrow dock, dandelions, poke, etc. We went back down the hill and turned into the gate and stepped onto the board walk. The tiny porch had an old leather couch on the left side and an old wooden chair and a big wooden box on the right. These pieces took up most of the space.

I don't remember if I was invited in or not, but I followed Alice through the door. We were in the big room. It was probably twelve by fifteen feet. Just to the left inside stood a double bed. It took up all the space in that corner. The open front door bumped against it. At the foot was another double bed with the headboard against the kitchen wall. Between the tall footboards was just enough space for her treadle sewing machine. It sat under a long window, with a view towards the highway.

Their front room, like their kitchen, was spic and span. It was obvious that Alice Baker, like most other housewives in Poole, was a good housekeeper.

To the right of the front door sat a small wooden table and two chairs. This is where they ate all their meals. In the center of the long wall on the right stood a small pot belly stove and a bucket of coal. In the northeast corner of the room were an old trunk and boxes that took up all the space to the kitchen door.

The cabin walls were papered with newspapers and pictures from magazines. Nails were driven in the walls behind the beds and over the trunk and boxes for clothes to hang. The house had no closets. On the wall behind the stove, Alice had hung all her pretty things. There were several small objects, but the only thing I remember distinctly was a beautiful valentine. It was the fanciest I had ever seen. It was pulled open to show a scene in three dimensions with figures of people, cherubs, flowers, and a lot of lace and ribbon.

Near the ceiling behind the stove pipe hung a large poster picture of the famous Dionne Quintuplets. They were pretty baby girls, a few months old, sitting in a row. They were the first known set of quintuplets to survive more than an hour. Every time Alice looked up at that picture she would shake her head and say, "I don't know how she did it, five babies at once. I just don't know how that woman did it." Of course I didn't know how she did it either. I had no idea what Alice was talking about.

By the next spring we had become such good friends that I went down to help them plant their garden. They had spaded the entire square of ground with shovels. There was a small square between the outhouse and the northeast corner of their lot that they had reserved for a little garden all my own. They let me sprinkle radish and lettuce seeds in rows.

Alice's green onions came up before ours did. I could see them just inside the front fence. I ran back to our house for one of Mama's cold biscuits and took it back to the fence. I reached through the wire and pulled a nice fresh green onion. I loved them with bread. I stood there in the gravel road and munched away at my 'snatched' snack. I was still too young to know I shouldn't pick things from other people's property. I thought they would want me to have it.

When their new potatoes came in, Alice called me out of my yard and said, "I know you like little potatoes with the jacket on and I saved you some." She sat me down to a plate of them at the little table, where I ate alone, enjoying every bite of these little brown balls with soft white centers seasoned in bacon grease.

Heck and Alice were the only people of a different race in town and I made no connection in my mind they were different except that they were old. To me they were just my friends. Years ago there had been three tobacco factories in Poole and half the population was black. There had even been a large rough lumber building at the back of Daddy's parking lot that was used as their church and school. It was torn down before I was born.

All the black population had moved away to find work. Eventually only this one couple remained behind, probably because they owned their own property.

I knew nothing about different races of people. I didn't learn about them until after I started to school. The closest I had come to knowing that people came in different colors was at Sunday school. We sang a song that went:

Jesus loves the little children.
All the children of the world.
Red and yellow, black and white,
They are precious in his sight,
Jesus loves the little children of the world.

I wondered where children this color lived. It must be on the other side of the world across the ocean somewhere, because there were certainly no children in my town any of those colors. We were all light brown, or near the color of some of the peaches that grew on our trees.

In my mind red was the color of apples, yellow the color of lemons, black the color of lumps of coal and white was the color of milk. I wondered what on earth people those colors would look like.

One morning Daddy said, "Dorothy do you want to take a short trip with me? I have to go out to the country and work on a colored man's tractor." Daddy was often called to farms in the spring and summer to repair farm machinery. He usually took one of us kids along. I don't know if he enjoyed our company or did it to give Mama a break.

I sat quietly in the seat beside Daddy thinking, "Oh boy! A colored man." I wondered what color he would be. In my mind, I pictured a man with stripes on his skin, every color in the rainbow. Or maybe he is one solid color, I thought, like those children in the song. He might be solid red, or yellow, or even green. I was happy as a lark. I was on my way to see a colored man.

We drove into a yard and stopped the car. The elderly man came out of his house and walked toward us. What a terrible disappointment. This man was not colored, he was just older and dark brown like Heck and Alice. My happy anticipation fell to my feet with a thud and slid into the ground.

I remember a few Christmases when we shared our Christmas treats with Heck and Alice. We didn't have the big Christmases that children have today, but we did get a big brown paper bag full of fruit, candy and nuts, besides a couple of toys and the treat Santa put in our empty shoe boxes. We wrote our names in these boxes and placed them under the tree in hopes that St. Nick would be there.

On Christmas morning Mama would give us two of her old, worn, long, brown cotton stockings to fill for Heck and Alice. We stuffed them with an orange, an apple, maybe a banana, nuts, and candy. I loved to carry them down to the cabin where we proudly presented these long, stiff, knobby, grotesque legs to our neighbors.

We stood at the door long enough to wish them a Merry Christmas and Happy New Year before running home with happy little hearts, because we had done something nice for someone. As far as I know, that may have been the only Christmas they had some years.

During the cold winters when the days dragged on, I sometimes looked out the window, saw smoke curling from the two chimneys in the cabin, and slipped down there for a visit. I liked to sit in front of their little warm stove and watch Alice sew. I liked the coziness of the little house when snow was falling outside.

Heck would be inside now. It was too cold for him to go fishing. He sat there in one of the straight back chairs, tipped back against the wall, with his feet on the bottom rung. He liked to sit there and tease me about anything he could think of.

One day he even called me out of my yard to tease me. He said, "Come down here a minute. I want you to see my daughter." I went inside and sure enough it looked as if someone was there asleep in the bed. She was on her side with her knees pulled up and the covers over her head. I stood there wishing she would get up and play with me. I had known they had children and grandchildren. I remember Irma, Virginia,

Mary, and a son named Ernest T. Ritman Baker Jr. who had all moved away. I thought they were all grown though. I had seen Ernest T. a few times when he came to visit.

Alice walked over to the bed and said, "Jim, stop teasing her." At the same time she jerked back the bedspread revealing a rolled up quilt. She scolded him for playing a trick on me.

Heck was full of fun and liked to have a good time. Alice was a more serious, no-nonsense type. This conflict in personalities may be why Heck received numerous scoldings. Except for this one time, I never heard any of it, but Marvin did. It would irritate him because Heck was his buddy and he didn't like to see him subjected to her complaints.

One day Marvin asked, "Heck, how do you stand all that fussing?" "Aw, she don't mean half of it," he laughed. "Besides, I just shut my ears and think about something else."

Marvin enjoyed Heck's companionship. Together they kept us supplied with delicious fried fish. At times they went to a good fishing place that took two hours to walk there. Heck was crippled as far back as we can remember. He always walked with a crutch. Marvin had an opportunity on these fishing trips to hear his many stories. He said Heck had a wit and humor similar to the famous cowboy entertainer Will Rogers. And he had the patience to sit on a pond bank for two or three hours without a bite from the fish. He would say, "It takes longer for the big ones to bite." Quite often they came home with a few foot-long catfish and a dozen or two green sunfish (we called them pond perch) from the ponds - or bluegill, longear sunfish, bullhead catfish, and carp from local creeks. Heck's favorite catch, however, was big snapping turtles.

Heck and Marvin were together so much around the town and countryside that the older men nicknamed Marvin "little Heck." He never protested because Heck was one of his very best friends.

I can remember enjoying some of Heck's story-telling too. On summer evenings about dusk, we children would gather to sit on the boardwalk when the Bakers were out on the porch. The walk was a foot above the ground and just high enough to sit on with my feet touching the ground. The only story I remember clearly and in detail was the one about his plans to go to heaven. I remember looking up through the branches of their cherry trees to the clouds passing in front of the moon and trying to visualize Heck up there flying around with his new wings, for that is exactly what he was telling us. "I will be going to heaven one of these days and have wings like a bird. I will be able to fly over Poole and look down on everybody to see what they are doing. I won't have to do any work or be sick, and I will have all the milk and honey I can eat. I know this is true because it is in the Bible."

He must have known something the rest of us didn't because not long after that he passed away. A casket was brought into the house and placed in the corner where the trunk and boxes were, probably on top of them. It was black metal and had a thin white netting draped over the open lid. I remember standing there looking at Heck asleep, while strange people in the room spoke in hushed voices. I remember standing in the vestibule of a small church with Daddy during the funeral, because there was no room to go inside.

Heck was buried in Shady Grove cemetery in the oldest section near the back fence and the road. I would go there often with Alice to put flowers on his grave. One day something happened to make this visit different than all the rest.

We always took the back road past the Fulcher family's house and Mama's old school site. After we ran out of gravel and entered the narrow dirt lane near our blackberry thickets, the road dipped to a low place where torrential rains had made such deep ruts that it was impassable by vehicles. There were only tall, narrow ledges to walk on. Trees and bushes grew thick on each side to form a tunnel. Tree branches overhead, including wild plum trees, made a shadowy canopy that blocked out the sunlight. We passed through this spooky place just before we went uphill again to the cemetery road. Then we followed a winding path through the cemetery. Alice would place her handful of flowers on the grave that she picked from her yard. She had plenty since her entire yard was nothing but flower beds and dirt paths and the strawberry bed. There was no grass to mow. All of the ground on the east side of the cabin to the vegetable garden was picked clean by her chickens. Sometimes we gathered wildflowers growing along the ditches to add to her home grown ones.

Heck's grave had a small homemade concrete headstone. The name and dates were written in with a stick while the cement was still soft. Alice would sometimes find the stone tumbled from its base. On this day we found it broken in half. She took a big rock from the ditch and propped it back up as best she could, wondering out loud how anyone could be so mean. I wondered too. Then she would begin her conversation with her dear departed and tell him everything she had done since her last visit. I would stand by patiently and wait for her to finish.

A summer storm moved in suddenly from the west. The wind began to blow and the sky quickly darkened. Alice was oblivious to all this as she continued her chat. "I will soon be coming to join you," she said. "Jesus is coming any day now to lift me into heaven where we can be together forever."

I looked up at the rolling clouds and knew that heaven was not far away. I knew that all the people who had gone to heaven before us were now living on top of the clouds. I had seen pictures in Sunday school of the angels walking on this fluffy white surface.

The tall cedars around the graves were really beginning to sway now. The sky was charcoal grey. Gusts of wind on the ground were scattering the flowers and tumbling them around. Alice paid no attention. She continued to tell him how she wished Jesus would take her soon because she was ready and waiting. "He's coming any day now," she said.

The sky grew darker. The wind blew stronger and bowed the tree tops nearer the ground. Oh, my goodness! I thought. Jesus is coming for her now and he might accidentally take me too! I knew I wasn't as eager to get to heaven as Alice and certainly not this very moment.

I had a sudden compelling urge to be at home. My legs got the message to run and they took off toward the church like a scared rabbit. I followed close behind. I had instinctively avoided going back through the spooky tunnel, but this route took me the entire length of all three cemetery sections. I straightened the winding path by going across graves. I knew I should never step on someone's grave, but no one had said anything against leaping over them.

When I reached the church, I followed the concrete sidewalk around it to the main walk along the highway. After I passed the school house, I began to feel safe because there were houses between there and home. It had begun to sprinkle before I left Alice. By the time I reached the church, there was also thunder and lightning. To be five and one half and alone in a thunderstorm at the edge of the cemetery was a frightening

Shady Grove General Baptist Church.

experience. I had never before been near the church and school when they were empty. The silence was eerie. As soon as I reached the path at the corner of our hill, I headed straight for the front bedroom and hid under the bed.

I lay there listening to the rain; it was coming down hard. I could hear the swoosh of the big branches in the locust trees as the wind tried to whip them from their trunks. I was safe now and could think. I was sure Alice was in heaven having milk and honey with Heck.

I don't know how long I lay there afraid to come out. Finally, I heard voices at the back door. Mama was talking to someone. I heard pieces of conversation. Mama said, "No, she's not home." Then I heard the other voice. "Looked all over, Direthy gone." My heart jumped to my throat. It was Alice; she hadn't left after all. She was back home. Then I realized they didn't know where I was, so I thought I had better come out of hiding. I crawled out from my refuge under the bed and went to the back door.

Poor Alice, her hair and clothes were plastered to her body. She looked like she had fallen in the creek and drowned. When she saw I was safe, she turned towards the back path to squish home in her drenched, floppy shoes.

Mama turned to me. "I'll declare Dorothy, what made you run away like that? You ought to be ashamed. You had Alice scared to death. Poor thing looked all over the cemetery for you. I'll declare I don't know what to do with you sometimes. You ought to be ashamed of yourself."

Poor me. It seemed I couldn't get through a whole week without needing to be told this. I think I may have spent a lot of my childhood either being ashamed of myself or pretending to be.

That fall I started to school in the first grade, just before I turned six in October. Our school never had a kindergarten. I loved school. It opened up a whole new world for me, and I found a room full of friends. My best friend was Doris June Stinnet because I already knew her. Her mother, Ruby Brown Stinnet, and my mother were first cousins and also close friends. Doris June and I were pleased that we had the same first two initials and our last initials stood side beside in the alphabet.

On the first afternoon of school, Miss Virginia Fulcher made us spread newspapers on the floor for a nap. We spread ours under the teacher's desk, thinking we would be out of sight and could talk and giggle. But it didn't work. Miss Virginia caught on to our trick right away and put a stop to it.

It was not long after that that I had another reason to go to the cemetery. Doris June was killed getting off the school bus, when a car struck her as she ran across the highway toward her grandparents' house, south of Poole. She and her family lived with Mama's Uncle Charlie and Aunt Lou Brown. After that sad event, I knew why I had never been allowed to set foot in the concrete strip that ran north and south so near our front yard.

Doris June had two older brothers, Jimmie and Jackie, but she was their only little girl.

Many years later I visited her grave with my husband and youngest son, John. I was shocked to see how small her grave was; then I remembered she was only six when it took one minute to snuff out her life and dreams, and the dreams her parents had for her.

As early as the first grade, we were making plans for the future. We would buy houses side by side when we grew up and were married. And we would share a convertible car. This is the kind of car rich people drove and we knew we could not each afford to buy one, so we would share.

I realized all these dreams except for the convertible, and as I stood there, looking down at my little friend's grave, I felt a little guilty because I had lived and she hadn't.

Now that I was in school, I could go to my cousin Mary Ann's house to play. I was big enough now to follow the path from my back door on through my grandmother's back yard and into her big yard just beyond Mama Russell's well. I had a new playmate and didn't go as often to visit Alice.

But every time I saw her heading toward the mill with her coal bucket, I would ask Mama if I could go. I knew she was going there to scoop up spilled corn for her chickens, and I liked to help her do it. A square door in the wall of the mill was there, high above the ground, for the trucks to back up to. The men would shovel corn from the truck and throw it into the mill through this hole, but they couldn't do it without losing some. After working hours, when the mill was closed, Alice would take her bucket and a whisk broom and get a few free meals for her chickens.

One day when we were inside the house, I asked Alice about the two pictures that hung over her bed. They were large, oval, nicely framed pictures. One was of a young black couple in their Sunday clothes and the other of a young girl with a derby hat sitting on her short dark curls. She said, "One is mine and Jim's wedding picture, and the other is of me. The preacher stuck his hat on my head just as the camera clicked. It sure made me mad."

Another time when we had returned from gathering corn and had just stepped on the porch, Alice suddenly turned toward me and announced, "I am going to teach you to count to one hundred. Say one." I said one. "Say two." I said, "Two." On and on we went until we reached one hundred. I was beginning to think that number, that seemed unreachable, must be in outer space somewhere. Finally we finished. "There now," she said with a sigh. "I have taught you to count to one hundred."

Alice had little opportunity for schooling and had never learned to read or write. I knew that her mother had been a slave and her father was her mother's white owner. Alice had been given away at age five to another family to earn her own keep. All her life she worked at any job she could find. She took in washings that she had to do on the board. Mama sometimes hired her to iron or wash dishes. If she was there at meal time, she would refuse to eat in the kitchen with us and would eat alone at the little table in the back porch. She told Mama she would rather eat the way she had been raised. She obviously was well-trained in the rules of segregation.

When Marvin was a baby, Alice was afraid Mama was too young to know how to take care of him properly, and she came up every day to check on him. While she was there, she would ask if there were any 'fleedaddles' that needed ironing.

One day I was helping Alice dry dishes and was dumping the table ware into a jumble in a drawer. She would have none of that nonsense. She had worked in a hotel and had learned the proper way to handle silverware. Although the drawer didn't have dividers, she insisted the knives should be on the left, forks in the middle, and spoons on the right, and she took time to arrange them that way.

Alice had a pride that soared above her circumstances. She wanted people to know, or think, she had nice things. Sometimes when she saw someone walking down the road past her front porch, she would raise her voice so they would be sure to hear, and say, "Jim, where did you put your silk tie?" or "Jim, do you remember where I put my green silk dress?"

When I got into the third and fourth grades, I had more friends and more freedom and had less time to spend at Alice's place. She lived there alone for several years after Heck died, and then was moved to Henderson to live with one of her children.

One day when I was fifteen, Ernest T. and a woman brought Alice back to the cabin, maybe to get something or check on it, I don't know. I was all dressed up waiting for my date with Billy and was killing time walking around in the back yard. I had on a white peasant blouse with short sleeves, a multicolored striped taffeta skirt and my long brown hair was curled and combed to perfection, plus powder and lipstick I couldn't be seen without. Ernest T. pulled his little car up to the path at the edge of our backyard when they were leaving and called me to the car. He hadn't seen me for a few years and couldn't get over how pretty he thought I had become. He told me I looked like a movie star, and he would sure like to take me to his dance hall Saturday night and show me off.

Poor Ernest T. had innocently plucked the wrong chord for me. My strict Baptist upbringing that banned drinking, dancing, card playing, etc. took over my reaction and I proudly, but tactlessly, announced that I didn't go to dances. Ernest was a little crestfallen, but Alice immediately came to attention in the back seat. She sat up a few inches taller and quickly said, "Now see Ernest, I told you there are people who don't go to them kind of places and you didn't believe me. Now see, I told you!"

They soon drove away. I watched as the car turned onto the highway and headed north. I could see Alice's grey head in the little back window of the car. I didn't know it that day but that was the last time I would ever see her. A few years later, I heard she had been buried in the back corner of the cemetery beside her Jim. I felt happy for her because I remembered the day she had so intensely expressed her wishes to join him in heaven.

I remembered the last time I saw her and was glad that my last remark in her presence was something that made her happy. Maybe it made up a little for some of the naughty things I did to her. Having five mischievous, little white kids as her nearest neighbors may not always have been to her liking. We must have tried her patience at times, because she would get a little peeved and refer to us as, "Them little white peckerwoods." I imagine I was called this the day I put dirt in her wash kettle of boiling white clothes. Mama said she had to empty it all out, refill the kettle and start her fire all over again. I was young enough that I don't remember.

Whatever we did was done in ignorance and just the normal mischievousness of kids and was never malicious. Mama and Daddy would not have allowed it.

One day some boys pelted their front door with raw eggs. Jimmie helped clean up the mess, even though he wasn't involved.

I am glad I grew up in a small town, inhabited mostly by gentle people. Although my world was limited, I learned values that have greatly enriched my life. One of my most valuable lessons was how to evaluate people. I learned that tall, short, fat, thin, clothing, color of hair, eyes, and skin was only the packaging. I learned to look past this and judge people by what they did and how they treated others. I learned to search for 'content of character' long before the black leader, Dr. Martin Luther King, so eloquently expressed it in his famous speech.

I feel sorry for the egg-throwing types. If any of them reach the same heaven that Heck and Alice are in, I hope they will be asked to step to a back cloud while Mr. and Mrs. James Baker are in the front row, enjoying all the milk and honey they can eat.

If their heavenly flight pattern takes them over Poole, as Heck predicted on that summer evening so long ago, they will find their little town looking much the same. But they will see that the little cabin they no longer need has fallen in upon itself and is covered with vines and bushes and weeds. They will see that the white house on the hill is still there but the five little white peckerwoods who lived there have all grown up, married, and moved away. The strawberries were there for many years because I picked some while the cabin was empty. My boundaries have been expanded now to reach several hundred miles in every direction. Through books and the magic looking glass called a television screen, I have been across the ocean and to the moon and beyond. But I shall never forget my first tiny world with its cows and old houses, cherry blossoms and strawberries, pink roses, and friendly faces.

UNCLE TOM LOST

Way back in the late '1930's our tiny town was insulated from the complexities and crime of the big cities and isolated from their culture. We were tucked away in the rolling hills of western Kentucky, surrounded by beautiful farmland and dense woods.

A few of the sounds to break an atmosphere of otherwise complete solitude were the puffing flour mill, mooing cows and clucking hens, the clanking of a push mower on cool evenings in summer, and the sound of coal being shoveled into buckets in the winter. Crowing roosters woke us in the morning. Croaking bullfrogs and crickets serenaded us at night.

Another sound to hint of life there and prove we were not sleeping was the sound of hammering. A large percentage of this hammering was fueled by the elbow grease of my Uncle Tom Melton.

Many times, walking to and from school, I would see this tall, thin, balding man balanced high on a rafter, single-handedly nailing together another house. He had built several of the houses in town that he either sold or rented. These little houses could suitably be described as four rooms and a path. The path led to the outhouse. None of the houses in town had bathrooms or indoor plumbing until the end of World War II.

Uncle Tom was a self-taught carpenter and all-around handyman. He studied architectural and woodworking books. But when he got down to the business of building anything, he usually drew his own plans and improvised with the materials available. Much of his work was unprofessional, yet functional, long lasting and, well, creative.

He was a great salvager. He could tear down an old grey barn and transform it into a neat little white cottage, or on a smaller scale, take a large empty wooden thread spool, put a big nail through the center and presto! - a knob for a closet door.

There were few homes in the area that did not have a sample of his handiwork: a new porch here, an outhouse there. If a concrete sidewalk, wallpaper, or paint job were needed, he could do it. He was a familiar sight in town walking almost everywhere he went. Along with his toolbox he carried a twinkle in his eye and a funny story on the tip of his tongue. Every child in town was his friend, and if he had an adult enemy I never knew it.

Unless someone gave him a ride he was often seen walking on the edge of the pavement, miles out into the countryside, to visit family and friends.

When my husband moved here from Oklahoma at age fourteen, along with his parents and two younger brothers, they would often see him on the road. Billy's dad would always say, "That old man is going to get run over one of these days." But he never did.

Uncle Tom also built many pieces of furniture; tables, cabinets, beds, and chairs came from his workshop near his house.

One spring day after my aunt had finished her cleaning, he brought out a living room suit he had designed and built and placed it in the parlor. It was a stuffed sofa and matching chair covered in wine velvet frieze with a leaf pattern. I don't think it had springs. The back was tall and straight, the seat short and hard, you had to sit erect and stiff, but it looked nice in the freshly papered room with the starched lace curtains hanging over the clean windows. Many houses didn't have a parlor; there were only wooden chairs and rocking chairs placed in front of the fireplace in the main bedroom.

Uncle Tom was a central figure in my life until age twenty, when I moved away from Poole for good, with my husband Billy and sixteen-month-old son Bobby (Robert Wayne). Besides my father and grandfather, he was the man I saw most often.

I was a semipermanent guest in his home, since his only child, Mary Ann, was my first cousin and number one playmate. I spent most of the day there only going home at noon for dinner and again at suppertime to stay.

Once I asked Aunt Sook if Mary could play at my house. She said, "Your mother has a house full of kids and I only have Mary. If she goes to your house, then I won't have anybody." So I didn't ask anymore after that explanation.

Aunt Sook was one of Daddy's three younger sisters. Her real name was Lillie Jane, but we never called her that. I was told that when she was young she was not an eager worker. There was a lazy neighbor woman named Sook, so they began calling her Sook and it stuck.

The next sister, Lila Mae, was married to Milton White and lived in a little house of Uncle Tom's across a field behind his house. She had a little girl named Sammy Janet. Aunt Lila Mae was our post mistress (master) for many years.

Uncle Tom and Aunt Sook's house in 1993.

The youngest, Bidley (real name Minnie Veneda), still lived at home. When she was a baby, and Lila Mae was still young, she called her idley bidley baby. Later it was shortened to idley bidley; then the idley was dropped. Bidley later married Jesse (Roy) Thornberry and had three sons, Tommy, Jodie, Billy, and a daughter Anna Jane.

My grandparents, George Areli Russell and Sarah Ann Tomlingson Russell, lived between our house and that of Uncle Tom and Aunt Sook. They were called Uncle Real and Aunt Annie by many, Mammy and Pappy by their children, and Mama and Daddy Russell by their grandchildren.

Our four houses were situated on a square of land, roughly five acres, plus a separate lot where Daddy and Daddy Russell's garage was located.

Looking east from Highway 41, the garage was on the left of a gravel road that went up a hill, turned right, and ran on past Lila Mae's house to the cemetery.

Our house was on the right of this road facing 41. Then there were two empty lots. Next was my grandparents' house and south of them was Uncle Tom's house with a large side yard in between. All of this was fronted with a long concrete sidewalk, one of the few sections in town. Other places had rotting boardwalks or no walk at all. Part of our sidewalk that ran along a high bank in front of the empty lots had a square missing. Heavy rains had washed it loose and it came to rest halfway down the bank.

One day while riding my tricycle, I overturned trying to cross this gap and tumbled into the ditch with my tricycle on top. I tearfully crawled out with bloody, scratched, skinned arms and legs. Maybe this is why Uncle Tom preferred to walk on the smooth pavement instead of the town's sidewalks. It was probably safer.

Our front yards were full of great shade trees: maple, oak, black locust, and catalpa. The locust and catalpa trees had wonderful, fragrant blossoms in the spring. Behind the houses were large vegetable gardens, fruit trees (apple, peach, cherry, apricot, and plum), also a large pasture, stables, pond, hen houses, smokehouse, coal houses, and last and least the tiny outhouse.

When Mary and I were old enough we were allowed to explore all this, but most of the time we were kept in the yard or the house under Aunt Sook's watchful eye. One time we went to their hog lot to watch the pigs wallow in the mud near their little pond. Pigs have no sweat glands and they have to do this

Aunts "Bidley and Lila Mae"

Aunt "Sook"

George Areli Russell

to keep cool. Mary's mother found us there in the mud near the edge of the water. She spanked us both. We didn't go hog visiting after that. We also learned the old sows (mother hogs) could be mean and dangerous.

There were plenty of other places to play. We would often corral our little cousin Sammy, whose dark hair was usually pinned up in neat rows of long banana curls, to sing for us. She had a beautiful voice. Also, we could explore inside the houses. Mary's big house had two small rooms used like closets and full of old clothes to dress up in and other interesting things to play with. Our grandmother's house had a big closet under the stairs with rolls and rolls of Sunday funnies we could open and look at. Upstairs had a wide hall and two large rooms. This was a spooky place to me since it was where Old Red Eyes, the boogey man, lived. We were often told he would get us if we didn't behave ourselves.

One day we actually came face to face with him. We were in Mama Russell's kitchen arguing and the threat of "Old Red Eyes" became a reality. There he stood in the doorway to the back porch where he had just stepped from the front hall. What a frightening sight: a tall man in a long black overcoat and black dress hat. He had a dark, ugly face with a mustache and large red circles around his eyes. Old Red Eyes had made a live appearance. I was scared silly and didn't feel like arguing anymore. Mary and I quickly agreed to be good little girls.

Years later, I learned this was Aunt Sook dressed in Daddy Russell's old clothes and a Halloween mask that she had made out of cloth. The red circles were made with red embroidery thread. Even when I was older, the upstairs in that house had a spooky feel. Although Old Red Eyes was long gone, he had once lived there.

We sometimes climbed the ladders nailed to the walls in the stables and played in the hay lofts, where bales of hay were stored in stacks, to feed to the cows through the long winter months.

Next, we might play in an abandoned car on the tree lot. We took several imaginary trips in that old car.

Much of our time was spent in the play house Uncle Tom had built. It looked much like his big house, only smaller with one room and a porch. It had real glass windows, with little panes that opened. A large square one in the back opened like a door. There was a fake brick chimney on one side. The inside was papered with flowered wallpaper, and there was wall to wall flowered linoleum on the floor.

Uncle Tom had furnished it completely with pieces he had built: a table and chairs, a doll bed, a high chair for the dolls, and a beautiful little kitchen cabinet like her mother's. All this furniture was enameled white.

Every time we played there, we set all the furniture out in the yard, spread all the bed covers and mattress in the sun to air, then swept the floor. After we put every piece back in place, we sat at the table and fed the dolls, thinking what good housekeepers we were.

One day Uncle Tom came to the playhouse, bringing a pan of black walnuts he had gathered from under a tree somewhere, and had cracked open with his hammer. We sat at the little table and laboriously picked out all the juicy meats. But it was a tedious job even with the nut pick. Finally, we were finished and had filled her toy tin coffee pot.

Mary said we should divide them equally to eat, so she took one, placed it on the table in front of me, then one for her. Back and forth she would place the nut meats saying, "One for you. One for me. One for you. One for me." Finally, after much patience, they were divided.

In the fast-paced world of today, how many children have the time to divide, one by one, a toy tin coffee pot filled with nut meats?

Early one evening Mary Ann and I went with Uncle Tom to a back pasture to bring their cow home for milking. She had spent the day grazing on grass and sweet clover in a field far behind our school. We walked across fields and climbed fences. Once Uncle Tom held open two barbed wires so we could crawl through without snagging our dresses or our tender skin.

Finally, we found the brown cow with white patches and a cowbell and started back down a narrow lane towards home.

We then cut across a different field. What a pleasant surprise. It was full of daisies. Hundreds of yellow centered flowers with long slender white petals covered the sloping hillside. We liked to pull the petals off one at a time repeating, "He loves me. He loves me not," down to the last one.

Mary and I happily ran through the middle of this fairyland gathering handfuls of the beautiful wild flowers. Suddenly I became aware of the beauty around me and the quiet peacefulness of the moment.

There to the right was Uncle Tom leading the brown cow, the tinkling of her bell the only sound in the cool stillness of the evening. A gentle breeze was blowing the daisies just enough to make ripples across the field, as they bowed their heads toward the sunset. The western sky was a soft glow with streaks of deep pink, blue, and gold-edged clouds.

Although I was only a child, I stood and held this moment close, hoping never to forget it because I felt so happy and glad to be alive.

We got the cow home and put her into her stall, then filled her feeding trough with hay. While she was wallowing this around in her mouth and using her long hairy tail to swat pesky flies off her body, Uncle Tom sat on his little stool near her backside and filled a large pail with foamy white liquid. He used both hands to milk and would pause to give a twist to one hand aiming a stream of milk in our direction just to make us squeal.

After Aunt Sook strained the warm milk through a clean flour sack cloth, a pan of it would be set into the water bucket and lowered into the cold depths of the well inside their porch. The rope was stopped and tied tight just before the bucket would sink under the water. There it was left hanging until it had been chilled enough to drink.

Now our day together was finished, and it was time for me to follow the path behind my grandmother's house, then down the lane and along a garden fence, on between the orchard and smokehouse, to my back door and supper.

A few days later, life took one of those little unpredictable turns for the worst and slapped me in the face, or more accurately, I should say the rear. I was back in Mary Ann's yard that morning along with Jimmie and Annie. Tom had his old, early 1920's model T Ford, open-top touring car (that he seldom drove) out in the yard. That kind of old car was a curiosity even then. Uncle Tom decided to make a visit to a relative's farm a short distance south of town. Mary begged us to go. We all piled into the car. Uncle Tom cranked the engine and somehow maneuvered the car onto the highway. He didn't seem to know much about driving it.

We had a short visit at Mrs. Clore Melton's farm, then came back to town. It was getting warm. We were thirsty and Uncle Tom asked us if we wanted a bottle of orange pop. He received several delighted yeses.

Just at the south edge, across from our church, was Linger Longer, a little Saturday night dance hall where liquor was sold. We knew we were not allowed to go in this place. But it was the middle of a weekday morning, with one or two people around, and we were with Uncle Tom. There was a little snack bar near the front door, where cold bottled drinks and sandwiches were sold. Cold pop was a rare treat.

We were just ready to turn the cold bottle up for a long draught of this tangy, liquid sunshine when in walks Daddy. He is as mad as an old wet hen. Mama was worried to death about us, he said. She didn't know where we were. Daddy put us in his little blue Ford and took us home. One by one we were taken to the bedroom for a paddling and lecture. I couldn't understand what made Daddy so upset. Now I know about his and Mama's fears for our safety. They knew about Uncle Tom's poor driving skills. He had never seemed to get the hang of driving any vehicle not pulled by a horse.

Many times they had seen him come careening off the highway into his yard on two wheels still in high gear. He had never understood enough about the laws of motion to know one should slow down before attempting a right angle turn.

Another time, he took such a wide sweep, he crossed his lane and ended up in Mama Russell's yard, where he barely missed the well and crashed into the smoke house before he got stopped. He jumped from the car loudly exclaiming, "It didn't scare me a bit. It didn't scare me a bit."

Then there was a humorous time when, in this same open-top car, he went driving through town in the rain, holding a large leaf over his head. This couldn't have helped much to keep him dry. Mama said he just did it to make people laugh. I'm still laughing. Uncle Tom was a born comedian. In physical appearance he reminded me of Jimmie Durante with half the nose.

We didn't get permission from Mama to take this drive, but I put the blame on Mary anyway for asking us to go. It may be one of the incidents that triggered our hair pulling, kicking, slapping fights that would cause Aunt Sook to want to pull her own hair.

Aunt Sook got so fed up with us one day she threatened to have Uncle Tom build a little jail with bars on the windows to put us in, right next to the sidewalk where everyone in town, passing by, could see and laugh.

Our behavior took a dramatic turn for the better. When our anger would rise, a vision of peering through bars into laughing faces would pop into my head. It had a great settling effect.

I remember the Christmas Uncle Tom gave me the pig tail. Daddy's sisters and their families all lived nearby, and we always had Christmas Eve together. Just as soon as it was dark, we would leave home with our gifts. We walked Indian file along the long winding narrow dirt path that led from our back door to Mama Russell's back door. Whoever led the way held the flashlight, and I always made sure I was somewhere in the middle. I didn't like being the last in line because I could always sense some imaginary thing coming from behind.

Upon arrival we were greeted with the usual warm welcome: "Hidy, hidy. Come in. Come in. Pull up a seat. Make ye selves at home. We're jist so glad ye could be here."

My grandparents still had traces of an old English dialect that had been preserved by their ancestors in the isolation of the Appalachian Mountains.

We placed our small gifts under the cedar tree that had been cut from a field near the cemetery. It sat on a builtin window box to the left of the fireplace. In front of this was Daddy Russell's straight-back chair. He would be sitting tipped back, with his bucket-of-ashes spittoon on the left and the dresser with the old curved top radio at arm's length on the right. He was listening to Christmas carols and waiting for updates on the whereabouts of Santa Claus.

Old clock on the mantel ticks away the hours as we wait to open gifts Christmas Eve, 1948. Mama, Daddy, Sammy, Jodie, and Marvin.

On the right there were two double beds with tall wooden headboards that seemed to reach to the ceiling. They sat on each side of the door to the front hall.

We all took seats in a semicircle of chairs around the fireplace, or sat on the edge of the beds piled high with coats. Then we waited and waited and waited until time to open gifts. It would not be polite to run through the house. All we could do was sit and watch as more of the family arrived, then sit and watch some more as the pile of gifts grew larger. The thought of opening those packages was the single thing that made this eternity bearable for me.

After what seemed like a year and everyone had arrived, someone would announce, "Marvin you can start passing out the presents." This ritual began with him because he was the oldest grandchild and could read. This honor passed to Jimmie, then me, and so on as we grew older.

I usually received three gifts, one from my grandmother and one from each of my oldest cousins, Mary and Sammy. This year I had a fourth, a foot square box wrapped in pretty Christmas paper and tied with red or green twine. (We didn't have scotch tape and pre shaped bows or ribbon.)

I was surprised since I had never received a gift from Uncle Tom before. I knew about the nice gifts he gave Mary so I hurried to open it. Inside wrapped in a lot of newspapers was a pig tail, an ugly, brown, dried up thing he had saved from hog butchering time in November. It was very funny to everyone but me.

The next Christmas I took advantage of an opportunity to retaliate. Every fall when it was cold enough to preserve the meat, the three families had their hog butcherings to replenish their supply of fresh meat. The hogs were raised in a back lot, or out on one of our farms. Every part of the animal was used except the squeal and the bones.

I retrieved the skull after Mama had boiled it to remove the meat. I placed this ugly thing, with its empty eye sockets and grinning teeth, in a bed of white tissue in a box, then wrapped it just as pretty as Uncle Tom had wrapped mine. He was not as happy when he opened his gift as he had been the year before when I opened mine.

Then there was the Christmas Eve that almost became a disaster for Mary Ann. After all our gifts were opened and the paper carefully folded to be stored in Mama Russell's attic for next year, Uncle Tom brought out a large gift for Mary and placed it on the rug in front of the fireplace. She opened it and inside was another brightly wrapped gift tied with twine. Inside that another and so on until the room was full of boxes. Finally just as Mary was reaching the end of her patience, there emerged a small brown unwrapped cardboard box. This had to be it! Inside was a handful of crushed newspaper. She lifted it out saying, "Oh this is just paper." Thinking she had been tricked, she tossed it into the fireplace.

Aunt Sook came out of her chair like a bullet, grabbed the poker and knocked the paper out onto the hearth. She somehow managed to smother the flames. In the middle of the ashes sat a small, charred white box. Inside the white box was a velvet box and inside this was a lovely wrist watch.

Everyone gasped in amazement, both at the value of the gift and at how near Mary had come to destroying it.

Next came the grand finale to our evening. It was the same every year. Daddy Russell would rise from his chair, pull out his billfold, and pass out dollar bills to everyone in the room.

Meanwhile, one Aunt had disappeared into the dark kitchen, emerging with a platter in her hand. It was piled high with squares of fudge, always the same two flavors, chocolate and peanut butter. I could have eaten half of it had I not been shackled with restrictions. Always, before we went to someone's house, Mama would give instructions on how she expected us to behave. I knew it would not be polite to take more than one piece so I had the agony of choosing. Sometimes, if there was plenty left, the plate was passed again, and I had the ecstasy of having both flavors.

After Uncle Jesse joined the family, he would go outside and set off a Roman candle. Then we found our coats in the piles on the bed, gathered our gifts, said good byes, and followed the dark path through the cold crisp air to our house.

Inside we would quickly inspect our gifts. Every year, until I was a teen, my gift from Mama Russell was cotton print yard goods for Mama to make into a new dress. The other gifts were usually a puzzle, paper dolls, or a coloring book. These gifts were very special because Christmas was the only time of year we received toys we didn't make ourselves.

Marvin with one of our many cedar Christmas trees that were cut from fields behind the school. Check out that fancy suit.

We had to go immediately to bed and to sleep. Santa could not come as long as one eye was still open.

I will never forget the Christmas I was nine. A shadow of gloom hung over the town. On December seventh the Japanese had attacked Pearl Harbor, an American military base in the Pacific. And we were officially drawn into World War II. Although the war was fought in strange lands far across a big ocean, the effects of it reached deep into the hills of Kentucky and found us. It brought dramatic changes into our lives.

New children began appearing in school. The government was forcefully buying land east of Morganfield and a few miles west of Poole to build Camp Breckenridge. Entire families were being relocated, many against their will.

One little town named Herman Valley was completely obliterated. This is where my grandmother (Mama Brown) had lived with her family before she married Papa Brown and moved to the farm where Mama was born. Her brother Charlie Duckworth still lived there with his family until they were forced to move.

I remember visiting them many times in Herman Valley. We had to cross a bridge with a wooden floor that sounded like every board was loose. It rattled terribly when we drove across.

Many years later Marvin went there to search for any remains of the town. It was gone. There was nothing left but a large empty field. He accidentally stumbled upon an old cistern he recognized. Now it all came back, and he knew where he was.

We began getting new neighbors and friends, but the draft was taking many of our young men. By the time it was over, I saw four uncles, one brother, plus several cousins and older schoolmates in uniform.

There was a flurry of activity at Camp Breckinridge. Much building had to be done to house the new recruits coming from around the country. Fun-loving young boys must be trained and transformed into fighting men.

A call for carpenters sent several men from Poole off to do battle with their hammers. Uncle Tom was one who went. Marvin also worked there a while until he joined the army at age seventeen and went to Ohio State University at Columbus to receive officer's training and an engineering education.

Rationing began, and we had to use stamps for things like gas, tires, and sugar. People were encouraged to plant Victory gardens to help feed themselves. We already did that. We were told to scrape carrots instead of peeling them. Nothing should be wasted. We gathered pods from milkweed plants. The fibers were used to make parachutes. Fats and oils were saved by the spoonful.

We saved our dimes to buy stamps to fill little books that could be exchanged for a twenty-five dollar war bond. Daddy bought a bond every month. Many men and some women went to Evansville to build airplanes and ships. We all pitched in and did what we could. There was an evil man in Germany named Hitler who was planning to take over the world, and he had to be stopped. I rehearsed a speech in my mind just in case I ever met him. I honestly believed I could convince Hitler he was wrong and get him to change his mind. (Oh, the innocence of youth).

All our soldiers came home from the war. I don't remember any casualties. Ironically, one was killed in a traffic accident while home on leave. He was the son of a farmer, Wayne Poole, who lived east of town.

We had a cousin, Ivan Russell, who was captured by the Germans and held prisoner for a long period. He lived directly across the road from Uncle Tom. His father, Roy Russell, was the banker and his mother, Mrs Delia, was one of my school teachers. Her niece, Ann Bruce, who lived with them and later became an adopted daughter, was Mary's and my best friend.

The day Ivan returned was a red letter day for the entire town. Almost everyone passed onto his front porch that day to see him and welcome him home. While he was a prisoner, he became like everyone's son, and they were all so happy and relieved to have him back. He married Lucy Powell, who also worked in the bank and had been living with his parents during this difficult time. He became the county school principal. They had two children.

His younger brother, Kenneth, married Lucy's younger sister Louise. They were two of the most beautiful girls I had ever seen.

One cold, snowy night, Uncle Tom and Aunt Sook saw three servicemen across the road from their house. They were hitchhiking and there was very little traffic. They invited them in and fed them a hot supper and put them to bed for the night. This caregiving is typical of the kind of people who lived in Poole.

Bad weather usually moved in from the west and whenever we heard a low rumble from that direction we would say, "Is that thunder or just the guns at Camp Breckenridge?"

During the war, many people expressed their dreams for the future. These dreams were always dependent on the war ending.

"We are going to buy a new car, when the war is over," some would say. "We are going to move to Florida, when the war is over," others would say. "We are going to build a new house, when the war is over," many would say.

Mama and Daddy's dream was the third one. They wanted to build a new house. Their growing family needed more room. The war ended in August 1945. By spring of 1946, they had decided that, since materials were still hard to get, they would just expand and modernize the house we already had.

They made their plans and hired a carpenter. Guess who? You are right. It was Uncle Tom. He came down bright and early every morning with his toolbox and that indispensable hammer.

He tore off the little side room where Marvin and Jimmie slept and the small enclosed porch across the back of the house. Then he built a big new kitchen and bedroom with a bath and short hall in between. Next he literally raised the roof, opening it at the peak to add several more feet to the height. This made room for two large bedrooms upstairs. He removed the old double dormer (we called the dog house) because it had always leaked.

Obviously, we couldn't live in the house during all this reconstruction, so Mama moved us into the little three-room building attached to the north side of the garage.

In years past it had, at times, been Mr. Brame's barber shop, Mr. Denning's grocery, Uncle Eugene's radio repair shop, a branch of the public library out of Dixon, and, during periods it was empty, a Saturday night meeting place for local musicians. Mr. Scott, a local farmer/music teacher, was usually in charge of these sessions.

Much pleasant string picking, fiddle sawing, foot stomping music reverberated off those old walls. When the building wasn't available, we went to Mr. Scott's house out in the country.

In the future this building was to become Mama's (Edna's) Gift shop and a gathering place for the Ladies Aid Society to do their quilting and catch up on local gossip (oops! I mean news).

But for now it was to become a shelter for the Russell family refugees. It had been empty for a long time. It was run down and dirty. We swept and scrubbed it thoroughly, then moved in the necessities: beds, a table and chairs, a gas range, and kitchen cabinet. In the back room, which had rotted boards we had to walk around, we placed the wash table, with a bucket and dipper and wash pans, near the back door. The well we shared with Alice Baker, the only black woman in town, was at the back on the opposite side of the garage near her cabin.

Mama cheerfully announced, "We will pretend we are camping; it will be fun." This camping adventure went right on through all the hot summer months. School started; we were still there. In October I became fourteen; we were still there. There had been so many unexpected delays. Finally, just before cold weather had a good grip, we moved into our new house.

I had never felt so rich. The old kitchen had become a dining room. We furnished it with a beautiful old second-hand dining room suit that Mama had found in Evansville and had refinished in mahogany.

She had her brother, L.D., build a bench to hold her house plants. She placed it in front of the double windows covered with ivory venetian blinds and new rose-patterned drapes (an unspeakable luxury). The room was so beautiful. The new kitchen had one fifteen-foot wall filled with white, enameled, builtin cabinets and a sink with real faucets. Mr. Wilbur Collins, our school principal, who had a workshop and paint store in the building on the south side of the garage, built them.

There were two square windows with small panes over the sinks. Uncle Tom had installed them too low. They were level with the cabinet and we knew dish water would keep them spattered, so mama asked him to raise them. He put them near the ceiling. We didn't have the heart to have him do it over. I always had to stand on my toes to see out.

There was a water pump and cold and hot water tanks in the new basement. They were hooked up to two sources of water, the well and the cistern. If one went dry and the pump kept running, a flip of a switch would change it over. No more carrying in water and carrying out pans and wash tubs to empty into the back yard.

This fifteen-foot square basement had originally been the old cellar with dirt floor and walls. Uncle Tom poured a concrete floor and built concrete block walls. Along the full length of one wall from floor to ceiling he built rough lumber shelves to hold Mama's abundant supply of home-canned food. On the opposite wall were two faucets for the Maytag washer with the roller wringer and two rinse tubs. There was a drain in the corner with a shower head over it.

And now to describe one of the most special rooms of all, the bathroom. It was only the second or third one in town. While it was being finished, everyone passing along the sidewalk would stop in to see and marvel at this modern convenience. We even had linoleum half way up the wall with a painted finish that looked like real bathroom tile. How I loved taking a bath now. It was so easy to fill and empty the tub and have water that was already hot. Just a quick push on a handle took care of what we used to have to go to the cold, spidery outhouse for. The chamber pot Mama had always had to empty, wash out, then turn upside down to dry disappeared from atop the chicken yard fence post.

Now for the first time Jimmie and I had our own private rooms. Marvin had already left for the army. Linda and Annie had the new bedroom downstairs. I was so proud of my new bedroom. Uncle Tom papered it in a green, yellow, and white flower design I had chosen from his sample book.

Once, when I was about seven, he gave me one of these old books to play with. It was full of beautiful designs on heavy paper. I made rugs, drapes, bedspreads, and pictures for my homemade cardboard doll house. Then I cut paper doll dresses from it. I would lay my dress pattern, just so, over the designs to catch a stripe, a flower or border in the right place and would have a belt, corsage or pretty hemline on my dresses. I had the most elaborately dressed paper dolls in town.

I wonder how many miles of wallpaper Uncle Tom pasted on walls over the years. I saw him in several houses, with planks laid across sawhorses, slapping his homemade paste onto the back of long strips of wallpaper with a long brush. Then, carefully holding it to the wall, he would smooth it down with another long narrow brush, making wide sweeps with his long arm. Sometimes there were wrinkles when he went around corners and couldn't get it just right. Many of the old houses had settled and the walls were uneven. Anyway it was always nice to have fresh bright paper in a new pattern. This paper was not washable and had to be renewed often because of the smoky stoves and fireplaces.

Now it was time to furnish my new room. I got one of Mama's original old iron beds and painted it white. On this I placed a white hobnail bedspread. We took the old homemade cloth covered wooden quilt box up there. Then we ordered an unpainted dressing table from Sears and varnished it. It had a curved front with two little arms that opened out, revealing the three small drawers on the right side.

Mama bought three pairs of yellow organdy, pricilla curtains, two for the double windows and one for the dressing table. She took an empty nail keg, turned it upside down, and made a daisy-print cushion for the seat and added a floor-length gathered skirt from the remaining piece of curtain. A round mirror with a border etched with flowers was hung on the wall to complete this arrangement.

How beautiful my room was. It looked like a movie star's room to me. I had a closet with three shelves on the left side. It held everything I owned, including clothes and shoes with plenty of space left over.

If you took a girl today, from a middle-class home, away from all the things she owns and put her in that room, she would think she was Cinderella before the fairy godmother paid her a visit. In that day and time and compared to what I had before, I felt like Cinderella after she became a princess.

I felt like a princess everytime I entered this room and sat at my beautiful dressing table in my own private boudoir. I was a teenager now and beginning to be more aware of my appearance. I had a cosmetic and manicure case Uncle Eugene had given me when I graduated from the eighth grade. I would sit for hours in front of that mirror, experimenting with powder and lipstick and new hair styles. My long, thick, brown hair was half way to my waist, and I rolled it in rows of pin curls when I washed it. This made it wavy and bouncy. I had been told I had next to the prettiest hair in town (Louise Powell Russell had the prettiest).

I would look at my reflection from every angle, "Yes," I thought, "I am coming out of my ugly duckling stage. The boys will take notice now." And so they did, but not Billy DeGraffenreid, the one I wanted. He was a senior and I only a freshman. I would have to wait a year. He would pass by me in the hall or gym, always in a hurry, and never notice that I even existed.

I had to sit by and watch as he took girl after girl for a ride in his Model A coupe. Part of his popularity was the fact he was the only boy in school who owned a car. On the other hand, his looks and charms alone were enough to cause the girls to huddle in a corner during recess and discuss them, expressing a desire to be the next passenger in that car.

Sue Oglesby was the last girl he dated. Sue and I were good friends although she was a junior. I went to parties at her house and even spent the night. We would sit at her dresser upstairs and try new hair styles we found in fashion magazines. We chattered into the night, sharing our girl-type secrets and dreams.

We also were roommates at camp one summer. We had gone with a group from church to Santa Claus Land for a week to learn to be Sunday School teachers.

When Billy began to date Sue, I would see them go past my house in that car. And when I saw them sitting together at school, I was so jealous I thought my heart would break. My freshman year was a long year, but it finally ended.

In early May, 1947, I attended his graduation. At the close of the ceremony, the graduates lined up on each side of the exit. I shook hands with the line he was in. When our hands touched, a current of electricity traveled up my arm that would have lit a hundred-watt bulb if one had been on top of my head.

By the following Sunday morning, there had been a development that changed my life. Sue had begun to date James Powell, the man she was to marry. When she broke up with Billy, she tried to make it as painless as possible and told him how much she knew I liked him. She also encouraged him to ask me out.

So that Sunday morning after church, he came up to me and said, "Would you like a ride home?" The answer in my head was "yes, yes, yes, yes, yes." But all that came out of my mouth was,

"Yes, as soon as I tell Marvin." I went to find Marvin, who was home on leave, and said, "I won't be walking home with the rest of you today. I have a ride with Billy." I remember Marvin's exact words. "Good for you," he replied.

Billy stopped the car beside the hill, next to my house, to let me out. He asked if I would like to go to Christian Endeavor with him at the church that night. "Yes," I said. That night when he brought me home and walked me to the door, he asked if I would like to go with him to the youth meeting Monday night at the Methodist church. "Yes," I said again. And so it went; every date led to another.

One night, little more than a year later, I lay in my bedroom in the dark, with my hand raised to catch the ray of light coming through the window from one of the two street lights in town. By moving my hand back and forth I could make streaks of light dance from inside my exquisite new diamond engagement ring.

We had ordered this ring from Papa Brown's wholesale book. It arrived that morning and Papa Brown brought the package into town and gave it to me. I combed my hair, put on some powder, lipstick, and my jeans, then pedaled Jimmie's bicycle down the two-mile short cut, out to the DeGraffenreid house in the country, to deliver the package to Billy. I wanted him to have it for our date that evening.

When he took me home later that night with the ring on my finger, I was too excited to sleep and just lay in bed looking at it waiting for the rooster to crow.

During the first cold snap in the new house, our three new gas floor furnaces went on the blink. The man who installed them was called. It was freezing out and our only source of heat was the fireplace in Mama and Daddy's bedroom. The man came in from working under the house to warm himself in front of the fire. While he stood bending over and briskly rubbing his hands together to thaw them, Mama said, "Now aren't you glad I didn't let you remove my fireplace like you wanted to last summer?" He quickly answered, "Lady I sure am."

Billy and I were married July 19, 1948, and moved to a twenty-five dollar a month upstairs apartment on Maryland Street in

Evansville. My Aunt Ceil and Uncle Dalphon Brown lived on the opposite corner at Elsas and Maryland.

We never liked this place, because the bathroom and entrance stairs were not private. We searched for months for another apartment, but couldn't find anything we liked for less than forty dollars a month. Billy's income was thirty dollars a week at that time so moving was out of the question.

One weekend while we were visiting Billy's parents in Kentucky, Mr. DeGraffenreid said there would soon be a little house vacant in Poole because a fellow oil field worker was getting transferred and, "Oh, by the way Dorothy, your Uncle Tom owns it. He might make you a good deal."

A visit back to Poole in our '31 Model A on Easter Sunday 1949.

Uncle Tom and Aunt Sook got unexpected company that afternoon, and we sat on the wine velvet frieze couch, and discussed the rent. He would let us have it for twenty-five dollars a month plus utilities. We accepted.

We became so eager to move back to Poole that Mama moved her bedroom into the dining room so we could have our own apartment in the bedroom side of the house. Annie and Linda already were using my room upstairs.

We had to wait two months for the little house. About the middle of August we moved. This was one of Uncle Tom's barn-to-house transformations. He had torn down an old barn just north of the millpond for much of the lumber. This was also one of his four rooms and a path houses, complete with a spool door knob on the closet door. It was a cute little white house.

The previous owners had reluctantly left a vegetable garden that we had the joy of harvesting. There was corn, tomatoes, and blackeyed peas to go on the table every night. This garden ran beside the garage all the way to the ditch along the road in front.

It was bordered on the driveway side and all across the front of the garden with bright zennias and marigolds. Another type of flower ran across the full length of the front of the house. These brilliant flowers, set off by the blue September sky, were almost a traffic stopper.

Behind all this superficial beauty were a few flaws. The two wells had surface water, which made our water supply slightly muddy. We had to carry all our drinking and cooking water from Mama's.

Uncle Tom had green roofing on the back of the house and two-thirds of the way down the front, where he must have run out and finished with blue. (Remember, I said he was a great salvager and improvisor.)

The floor in the living room and front bedroom was new lumber, wide plank pine boards that we finished with glossy clear varnish.

For the first few months, the living room was furnished with only one platform rocker, small bookshelves Billy had built in school in the eighth grade, and the daybed Annie and I had slept on so many years. Mama had made two large pillows for it and ordered a studio couch cover that made it attractive.

One afternoon we were sitting in the living room admiring our shiny, clean floor when we saw a streak of bright light in the center. This seemed strange and we got on our knees for a closer look. Through a narrow crevice we could see sun shining on the ground underneath that was coming through an opening in the foundation under the back bedroom.

It was basically a shell of a house. There was no insulation, storm windows, or double floor. This could be a major reason we nearly 'froze to death' during the two winters we lived there. Our only source of heat was a Warm Morning coal heater in the living room.

The method for preparing the stove for the night was to get a good fire in it, cover it with more coal, then top it with ashes and close the damper so it wouldn't burn too fast and go out during the night.

The house got very cold with so little heat. We had eight quilts and blankets on our bed, which were all we owned. We could hardly turn over under all that weight. We could feel cold air coming through the mattress. I got smart and took two of the heaviest covers and put them under the bottom sheet. This improved our bed quite a lot, but it didn't help the water bucket. I had to chip ice off the top of the water with an ice pick so I could heat some in the kettle to wash my face and brush my teeth to go to school.

Yes, I was back in school. I had dropped out when I married between my sophomore and junior years. Many girls in those days planned to be mothers and homemakers and didn't have dreams of professions or careers like the boys. It was a prevailing belief that mothers could teach a girl all she needed to know at home.

After we moved into the little house, it was nearly time for school to start and I began to get an urge to go back. I had always enjoyed learning, and I began to think I might want to go to college some day. I knew they wouldn't let me in the door without a high school diploma.

I told Mama my plans. She said, "Talk to Mr. Collins. He may not allow you back in school now that you are married." I talked to him in his shop next to the garage. He said, "yes." So, the first day of school, I was in the gym for the opening ceremony, in my new print dress Mama had made, sitting with my old school mates as thrilled as I could be.

Our house Uncle Tom built from a barn. After gradutation we borrowed Billy's Dad's '50 Chevrolet and took a short trip.

Those two years we lived in Tom's little house, and I was in my junior and senior years in school, can go on record as two of the happiest years of my life. We had no money, but we had each other and our youth. We had few responsibilities and were out from under our parents' discipline. We could come and go as we pleased, and we did a lot of that. Our idea of a fun Saturday was to pack a big sack full of Spam or bologna sandwiches and apples (we couldn't afford to eat in restaurants), fill up our 1931 Ford with gas at Mr. DeGraffenreid's, and drive all day, exploring every back road and little town we could find in a radius of twenty-five miles.

During the time we lived in Uncle Tom's little house, we only had one overnight guest, and this one was unexpected.

One evening, not long after Marvin and Nancy were married, they came to visit me. Billy was working late at Sears in Evansville, and Nancy suddenly decided to spend the night with me since Marvin was going to spend the night in a corn crib.

He had just discovered that some of his stored corn had been stolen and he wanted to be there in case the dirty thieves came back for more. Daddy had let him raise a corn crop on the old Tomlingson farm that summer for extra cash.

It is a lucky thing for the thieves that they did not show up that night because Marvin was very angry. He felt that since he did all that work, the corn and profits were his.

Isolated incidences of theft were about as near as we ever came to a crime wave. There had been a tiny, ten by ten, one-room jail built somewhere on the hill behind the post office years ago, but was seldom occupied.

Mama only remembers one man who was locked up occasionally to sober up. He was a frequent drinker, kind of an Otis Campbell type like the man on The Andy Griffith Show, who voluntarily locked himself in the jail cell each week. Our town drunk was also a gentle soul.

If we had had an Andy Taylor and a Barney Fife, they would have had nothing to do but sit on the bench in front of the tiny post office with the postmistress and whittle, trying to keep time with her crochet needle.

In all fairness to my Aunt Lila Mae, her mornings were hustle bustle. She had bags of mail to sort and shove into the back side of the tiny boxes while eager early birds were already lining the walls of the small room in front, to chat and wait for their mail.

Other chores, besides mail business, were to sweep up and keep a fire going in the little potbelly stove in the back room in the winter. Her duties slacked off in the afternoon and she had idle time.

She was an intelligent woman, who liked to keep busy. No thumb twiddling for her, so she crocheted. Over the years she created many pieces of beautiful handwork which she either sold or gave away. My wedding gift from her was a set of white sheets and pillow cases trimmed in her lovely blue crocheted lace.

Now I ask, who but me could begin a story about corn and end with lace?

Uncle Tom could still be seen all over town painting, hammering or pushing his mower to the cemetery to do some trimming. We faithfully took our twenty-five dollar rent to him every month and had a pleasant visit. He was always doing something around the house if he didn't have a job somewhere else.

The only time I ever saw him idle was on Sunday, or when he had company. No one worked on Sunday. It was the Lord's day and a day of rest. With four churches in town, most people observed this as a day to dress up, go to church, then stay dressed up and have company for dinner or be someone's company for dinner.

Uncle Tom had a lot of work to do at home, a large yard to mow, and a large garden to tend. He raised huge amounts of food there. It kept Aunt Sook canning all summer. There was a section of the wooden underpinning on his house he could remove. On the ground he stored potatoes, onions, pumpkins, and other foods. Some of it he stored in the attic.

Every year during the last days of May, I would see him walking down the road past our house with a gallon of his freshly picked strawberries hanging from the crook in his arm. He was on his way to waiting customers who already had visions of strawberry shortcake dancing in their heads.

He kept the coal buckets full and carried out the ashes; some of them, along with corn cobs, ended up in our driveway, which was always full of ruts.

He had the ultimate in designs for his coal house. It was just off the hallway between the side porch and back porch, both enclosed. There was no going out in the cold and snow and rain to get his coal. Ours was dumped into the back yard at the edge of the bank near the gravel road and was in the open. In winter, the snow on lumps of coal brought into the house in coal buckets, would melt and form puddles of black water on the floor.

Uncle Tom also had a five gallon bucket sitting beside the cook stove in the kitchen to catch all the food scraps, bones, peelings, and even dish water. He carried this out when it was full, to pour into the hog's feeding trough. This was called slopping the hogs. All farmers did it.

After I graduated and while we were on a short trip to Lookout Mountain and the Smokies (a belated honeymoon), Mama and Daddy moved out to the farm into the Grigsby house. Daddy was getting tired of working from sun up till after sun down and not being able to sit down to a meal without someone knocking on his door. It was "Alvie, I need gas, "or "Alvie come look at my car, I want you to see what this noise is." Marvin overheard one man ask, "Alvie, what's wrong with a car when it won't run?"

When we returned from our trip, they told us we could move into their empty house rent free. Jimmie and Mildred were now married and living in the bedroom side. We couldn't pass this up.

I reluctantly said good bye to my first little house, but it was nice to live in the luxury of the big house, with all the modern conveniences. This was in June, 1951.

The following February our first baby, a little boy we named Robert, was born. Mildred's father died and they moved away for a while to stay with her mother.

Then the constable, Hayden Lee Townsend, and his wife, Betty Sue, wanted to rent the empty apartment. Since they had two little girls, Pam and Sharon, we decided we should move to the little side so they could have more room. Anyway, we were already building a new house in Evansville and would be moving soon. We had come full circle in our living quarters.

Finally, we moved into our half-finished house in June, 1954. We missed Webster County so much we returned every weekend to visit relatives, and there were plenty of those.

Jimmie and Mildred had moved back to Poole with their small sons, Junior and Larry. They lived in the old, two-story Dixon house they rented from Uncle Tom. It sat on a hill, between two of the little houses he had built. The one just to the south was the one we had lived in.

We visited them one day, and as we drove up the driveway, we saw a man on a tall ladder, leaning against the second floor wall, slapping white paint on to the old weather board.

I knew Uncle Tom was about eighty now and well past the age when most people had permanently attached a rocking chair to their backsides. The man smiled and waved. Could it possibly be? Yes, it was Uncle Tom. This man was just not going to allow himself to grow old.

I next saw him at Mary's house when she gave Aunt Sook a big birthday dinner. Then sadly, the last time I saw him was at the funeral home after she died. Uncle Tom was about twenty-five years older than her, but he outlived her a few years. On his 90th birthday Mama said he announced he was still a pretty good man and was looking forward to his one hundredth birthday.

Then one day something happened in this quiet little town where the people were still friendly and charitable, still practicing the Golden Rule and Ten Commandments they had learned in the four churches, and were still well versed in the moral values taught in the McGuffy readers. Something terrible and unexpected happened that caused shock waves to travel through the body and soul of every man, woman, and child in town.

Uncle Tom had been murdered. His body had been found on a Tuesday morning on the floor of his bedroom. The broken chair was nearby that had been used to snuff out the life of a kind, gentle old man, who had never harmed anyone. The officials came and conducted an investigation, not finding much to go on. Then Daddy, in his search around the house, found a button on the ground under the window that had been entered.

After intensive questioning of the townspeople, certain boys became suspects. Policemen went to their home and matched the button to a coat. Two boys were arrested and placed in a hot, upstairs cell in the Webster County jail.

A new school teacher, who had recently moved there from Chicago, with a few boys under his care, had rented the old Oglesby farm house where Sue once lived. He also took in some homeless local boys to care for them, he said. How nice, the people of Poole had thought, in perfect keeping with their "Love thy neighbor as thyself" values.

But they found out too late that he was a crook running a little crime ring. Big city crime had finally penetrated the town's insulation and harshly jerked it into the real world. The man was immediately fired from his teaching job and fined.

Uncle Tom was buried in the cemetery behind Shady Grove Church beside Aunt Sook, not far from the graves of my grandparents, not far from the fields where he had cut Christmas trees, picked blackberries, and pastured his cows. He still sleeps just at the edge of the little town he helped build.

His hammer was silent now. If only he had had it in his hand that Saturday night when those drunken boys had broken in. They had just left a party where they had heard talk of this rich old man who hid large sums of money in his house. They ransacked the place, but never found it. He had it hidden in his mattress.

Twenty years later, I still feel sad when I remember. Then I reach deep into my memories and relive a moment like the evening in the field of daisies bringing the cow home to milk, and I feel better.

Mary Ann

I like to think that I can see Uncle Tom and Aunt Sook walking hand in hand across the blue, pink, and gold streaked clouds in some faraway sunset, their ageless spirits clothed in a raiment of eternal youth.

Mary and I are both grandmothers now. The playhouse is gone. I am happy to report we have both conducted our lives in a manner that has never caused anyone to threaten to put us in jail again, since that summer day, long ago, in Uncle Tom's front yard under the big maple trees.

MY FIRST AIRPLANE SIGHTINGS

In the mid 1930's we didn't know much about airplanes. Few people in our town had ever seen one. Many families out on farms still came to town in a horse drawn buggy to do their all day Saturday shopping and visiting. Most of the cars on the road were Model A and Model T Fords.

I will never forget one day at noon while we were all in the kitchen eating dinner (the evening meal was called supper) when we suddenly heard the roar of a motor in the sky. "That's an airplane!" Daddy yelled. We all jumped up to run outside and got in a jam trying to get through the door.

We saw a small plane overhead and stood watching in amazement until it disappeared. My first sight of a plane! It had actually flown over our house! We could see it and hear it and knew there was a real live man in it. Until then the only men I had ever heard about that were in the sky were God and the man in the moon.

We all went back to the table and Daddy told us how much he liked airplanes and how as a boy he would have dreams about flying like a bird.

Then one day an even more exciting event occurred. Literally out of the clear blue sky, a pilot in pilot's clothing came walking into Daddy's garage to use the phone. He was wearing an aviator's cap with goggles and jodhpur pants, the kind that are puffy at the top and tight from knee to calf high boots.

He and another pilot were flying old planes to Ohio to junk them when he became separated from the other plane. He took out his map to study, and being in an open cockpit, the wind snatched it from his hands and blew it away. He didn't know how far he was from the Evansville Airport and became worried about having enough fuel to continue, so he landed on an empty stretch of Highway 41 just south of Poole and taxied into a parking space in front of our church.

The pilot paid Daddy four dollars to guard his plane and protect it from the curious crowd that had already gathered around it. In that day and time this event was about equal to having a U.F.O. land on your street a block from your house. All us kids squeezed into the little blue '37 ford and went to church in the middle of the week.

There sat the plane; I could hardly believe my eyes! It was a real test of my ability to stay inside my skin, I was so excited. I was close enough I could have touched it, but was afraid to. It was such a strange-looking thing with its long wings like a bird, big paddles called a propeller on the front, and one little wheel under its tail in the back. Daddy had trouble with one little boy who couldn't control his enthusiasm as well as the rest of us and kept rubbing his hands all over it.

The pilot came back. He had made his call, but he reported to the authorities that he had landed in a field. He knew landing on the highway was a violation and he didn't want them to know. Soon, someone from Camp Breckenridge, a military base near Poole, brought his gas. The problem now was to get safely back into the air.

Roadblocks were put at the church and at the first big curve south of town.

Daddy said, "I'm going to follow him," so we all climbed back into the car. He stayed frighteningly close to the plane and once when the tip of the right wing caught on tree branches he had to slam on his brakes. Then we were off again, faster and faster. I was standing in the back clutching to the back of the front seat. We were so close I could see the little wheel bumping up and down on the rough pavement. We shouldn't have been so close. I wonder what the pilot's thoughts were if he saw us back there.

Then the plane slowly lifted into the air. What was holding it up? It was unbelievable that something so heavy could be floating like that. Then high in the air it circled to the left to go north. The pilot waved and we all watched until we could see nothing.

It was a big thrill for everyone in our quiet little town that day, and no one who was there is likely to ever forget it. One who hasn't forgotten is my cousin, Mary Ann. When she read this story, she became excited and said. "Dorothy, I saw that! I saw that plane coming down the highway with its wings wider than the pavement. I was on the sidewalk, nearly to the school grounds (the school was next to the church). I was carrying Jodie and had Tommy by the other hand. I thought that thing was going to hit us, so I hurried with the boys to get into Mr. Watson's house."

About 1947 Daddy's dreams of flying became a reality. He took flying lessons and bought a beautiful silver Luscombe with a blue streak down the side. Part of the money he used to buy it with was a sock full of silver half dollars he had been saving for years and kept hidden in a closet upstairs. One day while Jimmie's wife to be, Mildred, and I were cleaning up there, we found it and wondered how much it weighed. It was too heavy to carry downstairs, so we took the scales upstairs.

Later Daddy traded the plane for a tractor when he bought the Cobb farm, where he built the big brick house in 1953. This farm had a large two story log house covered in white clapboard and a log barn that had been there during the Civil war. Behind this farm is the old Russell farm, where Daddy lived from age ten to twenty-one when he went to Kansas City to school. After he returned they moved to Poole.

Daddy enjoyed several years of flying. We spent many Sunday afternoons at Henderson and Evansville airports watching him practice take-offs and landings.

Daddy and his Luscombe

BARNSTORMING

The end of World War I put most trained flyers out of work. Except for a few mail routes there was little commercial flying. Many pilots bought small, surplus war planes and flew them to carnivals and fairgrounds where they offered stunt flying and rides for a small fee. Landing in farmers' fields near small towns gave this activity the name "barnstorming."

About 1935, I've been told, a barnstormer landed at Poole in Mr. Fulcher's field less than 1/2 mile east of our house. Word spread fast and almost everyone in town showed up. A holiday atmosphere developed and iced soda pop and lemonade was sold. Rides were offered to all, but only the bravest accepted.

Kenneth Russell was one who was courageous enough to fly into the space formerly occupied only by the birds. When he returned he reported that the farm houses looked like matchboxes and cars looked like toys.

A quiet housewife, Mrs. Lea Denning, was another who bravely stepped on board the plane. As she reached to close the door she offered reassuring words to her anxious husband standing on the ground. "Well, Jasper, if I don't make it back, supper's on the table."

THE DAY MARVIN SAVED ANNA LORENE'S LIFE

Our little town was a town that cared when a major crisis arose, such as fire, accident, or disease. On occasion, the entire town helped the victims back to a normal life.

I remember the time our family was at the receiving end of this loving generosity.

It happened on a cold, cold morning. Jimmie and I were in the kitchen preparing for school. There was a pleasant warm fire in the coal- and wood-burning stove in the kitchen, where Mama was cooking breakfast, and another one in the fireplace in the bedroom.

Mama had made Anna Lorene and me new floor-length, full-cut, outing gowns the day before. Anna Lorene was still wearing hers and sitting in her little rocker in front of the fireplace. Her back became cold so she arose and turned her back to the warmth of the flames. The draft of air that crosses the floor and rises up the chimney caught her billowy gown and drew it into the fireplace.

We immediately heard screams. I had just made myself a fried egg and biscuit sandwich. When I ran into the room with all the others and saw a jumping ball of fire, with only Anna Lorene's upraised hands visible, my sandwich became a flying projectile into the far corner of the room. My heart was in my throat.

Marvin was the first to react and threw her onto the floor. He knew what to do, because his class at school received instructions about procedures to follow in case of clothing fires. Mrs. Alma Smith Williams had volunteered the information in her English class only two months before. He was in the bedroom where he had just pulled on his coat and gloves to go to school.

When Mama heard the screams she ran into the bedroom. There was a frantic scrambling for bedcovers off the bed to throw over her. Their quick thinking saved her life and saved her face from being scarred like the rest of her body. Marvin used his arms and gloved hands to keep the flames brushed from her face.

Dr. Lynn, our country doctor, who lived a few houses away was called. Jimmie ran across town to the Young's house to get Gwendolyn, a family friend. When he arrived, he was so out of breath he couldn't tell them what was wrong. Soon the news spread and people came from all over town to help. Going to school was completely forgotten. The day grew into a flurry of activity. Mama slowly became aware of the egg sized blisters forming on her hands. She must have beaten the flames with her hands because she received severe burns on both of them.

The women who arrived to cook our noon meal (we called dinner) put Mama to bed. I remember Aunt Ceil spoon feeding her as she lay on the daybed in the corner of the room. This bed was opened at night for Anna Lorene and me.

It took six months for Anna Lorene's burns to heal. Dr. Lynn decided to keep her at home during this period so she could be near the love and care of her family. Not much could be done in the hospital for burn victims in those days that couldn't be done at home.

They put bandages and an ointment called unguentine on her burns, which had to be changed daily. A man in town, Emmit Thornberry, brought his accordion every day and played music to take her mind off herself during this procedure.

Dr. Lynn told Daddy he knew he was not a drinking man but Anna Lorene would benefit from whiskey for the pain and advised him to get some. My Uncle Delmer Brown overheard this conversation. Knowing Daddy would not want to be seen in a liquor store he said, "Alvie, I will go get it for you."

Now the endless stream of well wishing visitors began. Day after day people were in and out of the house bringing small gifts, prayers, and words of encouragement.

Mama's former music teacher and close friend, Georgia Dixon, gave her own girlhood collection of Fritzy Ritz (a cartoon character) paper dolls. They were the largest, most beautiful paper dolls I had ever seen. Nickels, dimes, and half dollars

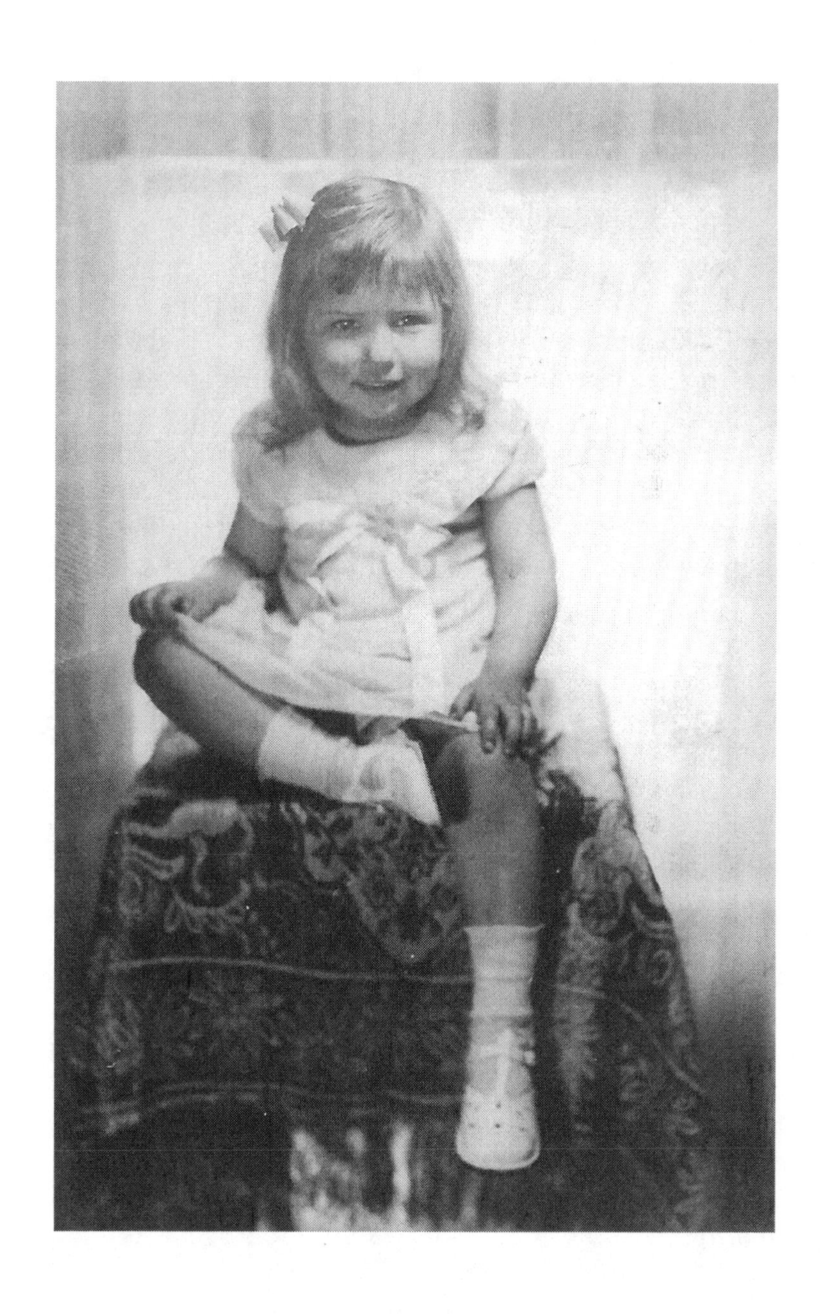

Anna Lorene

began to appear on the mantle, along with many other small gifts.

As the days wore on, I seemed to be getting more and more underfoot of the women working in the house. (It was a good while before Mama could use her hands.) Everywhere I went people would shoo me to another room, or outside where I could sit on a board behind the smokehouse and pout, or on the high bank in front of the house where I could watch the cars go by.

I was only seven or eight and the big green monster called jealousy began to raise it's ugly head. Anna Lorene was getting all the gifts and attention while I felt unwanted. Being so young I did not realize I would not have wanted to trade places with her.

One day the temptation of all those shiny coins on the mantle became too much for me. I took a dime and ran to the restaurant and treated myself to a double dip ice cream cone. The pleasure was short lived because I couldn't shake off the gnawing guilt in the pit of my stomach due to this terrible crime I had committed.

As Anna Lorene began to recover, she was able to sit in a chair. She had grown pale and thin. Her beautiful blonde curls were cut short and looked more like a small straw stack.

One day she began leaning forward in her chair, trying to see herself in the long chiffarobe mirror. She couldn't quite do it, so she said, "Mama I, want to see myself." Mama tried to discourage her, because she looked like a little scarecrow. She was wearing shabby pajamas and her hair wasn't combed. Mama was afraid that if Anna Lorene saw herself in the mirror, she would be frightened.

Anna Lorene was determined to see her reflection in the mirror. There was nothing we could do but help her to stand and turn her toward the chiffarobe. The image looking back at her from the mirror was enough to make even the strongest of souls cry.

At that moment the spirit of Anna Lorene became evident, the spirit that was behind her recovery. When she saw her reflection she viewed it as comical. Instead of being frightened she began to laugh. She burst into that full blast of laughter we are all so familiar with. She continued to laugh for several minutes as if she had just been told the funniest joke in the world.

Along with her spunky spirit she also had a strong faith in Jesus. She firmly believed he would heal her and asked people to pray for her.

She eventually recovered with all her arms and legs and spunky spirit intact. Dr. Lynn told us later that he had lost patients with fewer serious burns than hers and did not in the beginning have hope for her recovery. At one point there was fear she would lose one leg.

Marvin

Marvin is a modest man and resists praise, but the facts are there. If he had not still been home that morning, this would have been a different story. Yet he insists that Mama, Mrs. Alma Williams, and God deserve much of the credit.

Annie's laughter is still ringing over the hills of Kentucky, fifty years later.

MY PLAYHOUSE UNDER THE ROAD

It was spring, I was nine years old. My older brother Jimmie and I had come home from school. After we listened to "Jack Armstrong" and "Terry and the Pirates," on the radio (we had never heard of television), we decided to go down and play on the boardwalk just beyond Daddy's garage.

Daddy worked all day in the back of this big building repairing cars. My grandfather stayed in the office up front to put gas into empty tanks when cars stopped at the two pumps out front.

After the customers were gone, he would lean back in his chair against the wall. His chair sat between a pot belly stove and an old roll top desk piled high with dusty books and a water bucket. The bucket held a dipper everyone could drink from. He sat in that chair much of the day, coaxing scratchy, squawking sounds from his fiddle. He must have had different ears than the rest of us because he seemed to enjoy his music. People would ask Daddy how he could listen to that all day and he would say, "Oh, it don't bother me none." I am told he entertained people with pleasant music from his guitar and banjo, but he never could get the violin to cooperate.

The board walk was a fifty-foot span that crossed the creek beside the garage and ran along a big ditch next to the road. Years of exposure to the weather had caused the supporting posts to rot and sink into the ground at different levels. This twisted the walk and made it wavy like a roller coaster. We liked to run up and down the slanting wooden hills and try not to fall off.

After we grew tired of this, Jimmie said, "Let's play in the culvert." He jumped off the walk and scrambled through the creek. I followed him.

What a wonderful place to explore. It was a long concrete tunnel with a flat floor and ceiling. I could easily walk through, but Jimmie had to duck his head a little.

The culvert today - 1993. It is half filled with mud.

At the far end, there was a small pool of water. We walked on the edge of the concrete to go around it and found ourselves at the bottom of a deep creek that ran between the mill and the mill pond. It looked like a little canyon with trees teetering on the rim, held there by gnarled roots sticking out from the sides of the bank. They looked like a tangle of snakes. I decided to go back into the tunnel.

While standing there in the middle of the floor, I was suddenly struck with an idea! What a great place to put my play house! I knew I was never going to get a real wooden one like my cousin, Mary Ann had, with glass windows that opened, flowered wallpaper, and a little front porch like the big houses. I had given up begging for it a long time ago.

This place didn't have windows but it had a big door at each end to let in the sunlight. I ran home to get my green wicker doll buggy. I piled it up with dolls and dishes. After I managed somehow to get it down into the culvert, I ran back for my doll bed and an old homemade table.

The bed was the nicest plaything I had. It was varnished a shiny brown and had a pink mattress covered with butterflies. My oldest brother, Marvin, and Aunt Tina had made the crooked little table out of scrap lumber years ago.

Next I got some boards and bricks out of the creek and built shelves against the wall for my dishes. These were chipped and cracked dishes Mama had given me from the kitchen, but they still had pretty painted flowers on them. I had fruit jar lids for pans. Now I was all set to play house.

Every day after school, I would sneak off to my secret house to cook and sweep and push my dolls in the buggy up and down inside the long tunnel. At suppertime, I pushed my buggy and dolls home, leaving the rest of my things down there. It was too hard to move it all.

One night a storm moved in. It brought a long hard rain, a real gully-washing cloud burst, the kind of rain that caused us to have to put pans on the floor to catch the drips from our leaky roof. I thought smugly that my play house had a better roof than our house, because it was under the concrete road.

Next morning was Saturday and the sun was shining again. As soon as I could get dressed, I ran down to see if my things were all right. I was not prepared for the sight that met my eyes! I could hardly believe it! Three or four feet of water was rushing through that tunnel, roaring like a train. All I could do was go back to the house and wait.

When I returned the water was down. It swirled around my ankles as I waded in. The tunnel had been swept clean. There was not a sign of any of my furniture.

I ran to the far end and looked down the creek, but there was still nothing in sight. I followed the creek to a big curve, which was as far as I dared go, hoping to find my doll bed caught in some tree roots in the side of the bank. I didn't mind losing the other things, but that little bed was special. Santa had brought it on Christmas, when I was about three, and it was the only doll bed I had ever had, or was ever going to have.

I decided to wade into the pool and feel around for it. Instantly I stepped on a big piece of glass and cut a bad gash in the bottom of my foot.

Monday morning Mama said I was going to school, bandaged foot or not. I didn't know how I was going to hop a long block to school and back. My oldest brother Marvin came to my rescue and offered to carry me on his back. So I traveled piggyback a few days until I could wear my shoe again. Marvin was fourteen and strong, but I must have been a heavy load.

Me holding a doll that escaped my playhouse flood.

Knowing that creeks eventually empty into rivers, the next time we went to Evansville and crossed the bridge over the mile-wide Ohio, I looked to see, half afraid my bed would be floating on the surface and my parents would ask how my doll bed got into the river.

A few years later, I was looking in Mama's old wooden quilt box and saw a small folded piece of pink cloth covered with butterflies. I showed it to Mama. A funny look crossed her face. "You made that doll bed mattress for me didn't you?" I asked.

"Yes" she answered. "And your uncle Delmer made the bed." Now I felt even worse about losing it.

If only I had asked one of my parents if I could put my playhouse in the culvert. They would have said, "No," and saved me all that unhappiness.

Parents are wiser than children about those kinds of things. They knew why the long concrete tunnel ran under the road and I didn't.

From left to right: granary, mill, garage.

MICE IN THE WHEAT

One day after dinner, Jimmie and I ran out the door for an afternoon of exploring. First we inspected the boardwalk and creek. We walked through the culvert, checking our height against the concrete ceiling, then climbed the bank next to the mill.

Being near the mill usually gave us a need to check our weight also. Just inside the double front doors stood a tall scales for weighing bags of grain. It was fun to adjust the little weights and see how much we had gained.

In the back corner, next to large piles of bags of flour and meal was a wide, double flight of wooden stairs. We ran to the second floor, then to the third. Looking out the dusty window to the north, we could see all the way uptown. Looking straight down from our position in our sky scraper, we could see all the way to the bottom of the creek. This made us dizzy and we turned our heads away to watch the machinery.

In the center of each floor, surrounded by a guard rail, was part of the monster that provided the power to grind the farmer's grain. It was an odd assortment of large mechanical things and large whirring belts. It all quivered and puffed and chugged. Everything was covered with a powder of white flour. Large, lacy, white cobwebs hung from parts of the machinery and shrouded every corner.

Being alone up there suddenly became spooky. We ran down both double flights of stairs and out into the sunshine.

The scales at the granary next door were also a curiosity. They were ground level and large enough to drive a loaded truck onto. Above this was a door in the wall built the right height for emptying the trucks with a shovel.

We noticed the ground level door was opened and we peeked inside. We saw a large golden pile of fresh whole wheat grains.

What child could resist the temptation to play in it? Certainly not these two imps.

We knew we probably shouldn't play in the wheat so we hesitated. "You go first," Jimmie said. "No, you go first," I argued. The thoughts of sliding in that pile made the decision for us, and we both went first.

We climbed and crawled around in the sweet-smelling, shiny, little oval-shaped balls. We let handfuls slide through our fingers. I noticed the aroma and stuck my tongue into a handful to take a taste. It was chewy and delicious.

"You better not eat that stuff," Jimmie said. With deaf ears, I took another bite, then another.

Suddenly, my legs had an urge to tell Mama about this new food I had discovered. They took me flying across the highway and up the bank into our yard.

I burst into the kitchen where Mama was washing dishes and asked, "Mama, have you ever tasted whole wheat? It is delicious."

Mama wiped her hands on her apron and turned toward me with her hands on her hips. "Oh my goodness!" she said, "I hope you didn't eat too much. When I was growing up back on the farm, we used to find dead mice in the barn. They had gotten into sacks of wheat and had eaten too much. The wheat swelled up in their stomachs. They split open and died."

Boing!! My happiness level went from real high to real low, real fast. I was petrified. This news had a physical effect I could feel from the hair on the back of my head to my shoe laces. Would this happen to me?

My mouth suddenly became very dry. I went to the water bucket and picked up the dipper. "Don't drink any water!" Mama yelled. "It will just make those kernels swell faster."

I ran out the back door and sat on the old boards behind the smoke house. I waited for the end to come, for what seemed like hours, but was probably only minutes. I kept checking my stomach to see if it had grown. Nothing changed. Slowly I began to recover and ran off to play. I climbed the catalpa tree beside the smoke house. Maybe sitting up there would keep me out of trouble for awhile.

Views looking north and northwest from top floor of the mill.

MY FRIEND ANN

School days were over by late April or early May. Children were needed to help plant the big gardens and fields, especially the ones who lived on farms.

I stood in my yard this beautiful spring morning on the first day of summer vacation. The fresh air was filled with the sound of singing birds and the sweet smell of fruit tree blossoms and other flowers. What a wonderful feeling to be nine years old and to have the whole summer, with its long lazy days stretched out before me. I was free to do anything I wanted to do, after my chores were done.

While sitting on the edge of the bank under the locust trees, watching the cars go by, and enjoying the freedom of not going to school every morning, my friend, Ann Bruce, came walking down the sidewalk.

"Hi Dorothy," she said. "I'm going to Uncle Willie's house to play the Victrola. Do you think Miss Edna would let you go with me?"

It only took me a minute to get permission, and in another minute we were skipping past the gas pumps in front of Daddy's garage. Through the open office door, we could hear my grandfather plucking pleasant music from the strings of his banjo. Then we crossed an exposed beam at the end of the boardwalk to reach the section that remained. Every step across this wavy, slanted walk was a balancing act that put us in danger of falling into the creek. We didn't care; it only added to the excitement.

At the end, we crossed a narrow gravel lane that led to Uncle Willie's barn. Then we ran up the corner of a low hill into his yard. Uncle Willie Bridwell was related to Ann, but everyone in town called him Uncle. We ran past the cellar, which was a square hole in the ground with a little roof on top and steps down to its cool interior. Fresh fruits and vegetables were stored there during winter and summer.

We went around to the back door and walked right in. No one knocked in those days. The grownups might pause a moment and yell, "Hello, anybody home," then wait for the answering welcome, "Come in, come in," before they entered.

Uncle Willie's house

Aunt Annis was busy in the kitchen peeling potatoes. A smell of apple pie drifted from the oven. All over town, at that time of morning, women were in their kitchens cooking the big noon meal. Back then, women were taught that their place was in the home. All little girls knew that when they grew up, they would become a wife and mother and keep house all day.

We asked if we could go in the parlor and play the Victrola. The parlor was a large, pretty room in the front of the house. It was kept neat and clean for company. All the pretty lamps and breakable things were kept there on tables and on whatnot shelves in the corner.

Aunt Annis said yes, because she knew we were good girls and wouldn't mess up anything. We had played there before. Ann opened the bottom door on the tall varnished cabinet that was almost as tall as we were and pulled out the heavy disks. She chose one and put it on the turntable under a lid on top. Then she took hold of the hand crank and turned it round and round until it was tight. Something on it was broke, so she braced a ladderback wooden chair against it to keep the handle from unwinding. Once the chair slipped and that handle took off like a tornado. We had to jump back to keep from being hit.

These were very comical records. I think some were called "Uncle Josh". Those high pitched little voices sounded so funny. I loved going there to hear those records. We didn't have a Victrola at my house, just a radio. Television was unheard of.

We stayed in that cool shadowy room with flowered wallpaper, listening to the music for a long time. There was a cool breeze blowing the lace curtains. The morning sun was still at the back of the house and the maple trees shaded the yard in front.

Suddenly, we heard a noise out back. It was a farm tractor plowing the garden. We wanted to watch, so we hurried to put the records away, and leave the room as we had found it.

Outside in the garden, Uncle Willie was already there, sitting against the fence. Even though he was completely blind, he could go anywhere on his property he wanted to. He had nailed several clothesline wires near his back door and each one ran to one of his out buildings. They led to the well, coal and smoke house, chicken house, cellar, and barn. All he had to do was take hold of the one he wanted when he stepped out the door, then let his upraised hand glide along the smooth surface and in no time he could be there.

We watched the tractor as the plow blades dug into the soil and turned the sod completely over, leaving large, smooth lumps behind. There were pink, slimy fishing worms crawling everywhere, raising the head end of their long bodies to the sun.

Enough of this. We decided to climb the paw paw tree that grew beside the coal house and smoke house. It stood so close, the branches hung out over the corrugated tin roof. We soon discovered how hot the tin was. The midmorning sun had already made it too hot to touch. If we hadn't been wearing shoes we couldn't have stayed up there. "Hot enough to fry an egg," we had heard grownups say.

Then an idea popped into both our heads. We would fry those worms!

We scrambled down the tree, found a tin can, filled it with the wiggly, pink worms and got back on the roof. We carefully laid the worms in the valleys of the corrugated tin. There were long rows of them simmering in the sun. Soon we were thirsty and decided to go to the well for a drink.

Ann drew up a fresh bucket of water from deep down in the cool ground. Our clear drinking water came through a good filter of 30 feet of sand and sandstone. A gourd dipper hung on a nail inside the covered well. Every well in town had one.

A gourd had at one time been growing in the garden. It was like a small pumpkin with a long neck. A piece was sliced off the side of the round part and all the seeds and pulp were scraped out. Then it was washed and hung to dry. The long neck became the handle and was used to dip the bowl into anything. The early pioneers had learned how useful gourds were from the Indians.

After drinking our sparkling refreshment from the well, we climbed around in the maple trees in the front yard, then went into the cellar, got an apple, and went home.

Next afternoon we went back to check on our worms. They were curled and dried. They resembled bacon rinds and maybe that is why we thought of having another bacon fry. This was one of our favorite things to do.

We took time to run back in the house a minute. In the bedroom, Ann handed down a tiny bottle from the high shelf in a tall wardrobe and we had another look at Uncle Willie's pickled tonsils. Before we reached home we had made plans to have our cookout as soon as it was dark.

I told Jimmie about frying the worms. "You mean thing," he said. "How could you be so cruel?"

"Worms can't feel anything," I snapped back.

"They can too."

"Then why do you stick them on fishing hooks?"
"That's different."
"How is it different?"
"Because everybody does it."

"Well if worms can feel pain then you shouldn't do it," I scolded. "Just because everyone does it is no excuse; pain is pain."

Jimmy gave up. He was already learning it was useless to argue with his hard-headed sister. But it did cause me to think maybe I shouldn't have fried the worms. Well, I couldn't think about that now; I was too busy planning the next thing I was going to fry.

I had Mama slice a little pile of bacon from the big slab on the table in the back porch. I couldn't get it thin enough. I wrapped it in wax paper and put it in a brown paper sack, along with part of a loaf of light bread (this is what we called store-bought bread). Now, all I had to do was wait for the sun to set behind the locust trees.

At dusk I went to Ann's house. She had her bacon and bread ready, plus an iron skillet, a shelf from the oven, and a fork.

Ann lived with her Aunt Adelia and Uncle Roy Russell and cousins, Ivan and Kenneth. Her mother had died after her youngest brother Richard was born and the youngest three children were taken in by relatives. Her father kept the oldest son, Jimmy. An older sister, Ruthie, went to live in Evansville with their mother's sister, Margaret Young. Ann was taken by another sister, Aunt Adelia. The baby, Richard Allen, was raised by his paternal grandmother in Dixon.

Adelia Russell was a school teacher and Roy Russell was the banker in our only bank. All teachers were called Miss, whether they were married or not, so Ann's Aunt was known by most as Miss Delia (pronounced Deely).

My family called them Cousin Deely and Cousin Roy, because he was my Grandfather Russell's first cousin.

Back to the cookout. Ann took the flashlight and we went around behind the old Missionary Baptist Church. Ann led the way, and we followed a narrow dirt path through the weeds and across a ditch to the top of a ridge. Here stood large trees and a fence. Just across the fence, the tree-covered hill sloped sharply to a stream. We put the oven shelf on three rocks that were already there, gathered dry sticks, and soon had a hot fire and sizzling bacon.

As we sat on a log, I knew this was a moment to remember. The smell of the bacon mingled with the fragrance of the woodsmoke, moss, and decaying leaves. Sounds of life came from deep in the woods, and bullfrogs were croaking in the distance from a pond somewhere. We weren't afraid up there alone in the dark. These were happy familiar sounds and we felt very safe. We lifted the crisp slices into our bread and ate sandwiches until we were stuffed, then went home.

Sometimes my cousin Mary, who lived across the road from Ann, joined us. Other times we held our bacon fry at my house behind the smokehouse. Anna Lorene and her friend, Marilyn Shelton, became part of the circle around the fire.

Mama came out of the kitchen into the bedroom one day where Anna Lorene and I were playing with our dolls. She was holding two folded pieces of pretty printed cloth she had just washed and ironed. They were large squares that had been feed sacks for one hundred pounds of chicken feed. Farm women bought large amounts of this feed and used the cloth for dresses, aprons, curtains, and tablecloths. The material was similar to calico, which was a cheap cotton fabric printed with beautiful designs. It had originated in Callicut, India, which explains the name. Calico was a very popular fabric with country women for everyday wear.

Mama had removed the stitching from the bag so it could be laid flat for cutting. One was a small blue flower design, the other had large purple flowers. She handed them to me. "Would you and Ann like to have these to make gathered skirts?"

I took the material and showed it to Ann. She chose the blue print and we made our skirts and wore them to school until we outgrew them. We were so proud of these feed sack skirts we had made ourselves. Starched and ironed they looked as fresh and pretty as any of our clothes.

Ann and I went to different churches. She went to the Missionary Baptist Church next to her house, and I attended the

One of the houses built by Jerome Duckworth still stands south of Poole.

General Baptist Church. My mother's grandfather, Jerome Duckworth, built both of these churches, plus several houses in and around town.

When our churches weren't having services at the same time, we would go to both churches together. After our sunrise service at Easter, I could go to her church later that same morning. I went to B.Y.P.U. (Baptist Young People's Union) at her church on Sunday nights until our church began Christian Endeavor on Sunday nights. We also shared Bible School at both churches and the picnics that followed.

One time during a revival at Ann's church, the preacher made a deal with the children. He would give a nickel to all who would memorize a Bible verse and recite it to the congregation.

I got my name on the list and learned my verse. When my name was called, I was seated at the back and had to walk the entire length of the aisle.

While the preacher waited, he said, "Here comes a tiny girl, waddling like a duck." Everyone laughed. By the time I reached the platform and stood beside the podium, I was almost too angry to get through the verse. When the preacher held out his old nickel, I didn't want it. But a nickel was a lot of money. It would buy an ice cream cone with a big dip of ice cream on top. I already had visions of licking on a sweet, creamy ball of chocolate ice cream, so I swallowed my pride and took the nickel.

One summer, one of the teachers at her church, Maralea Arnett, took Ann, her sister, Ruthie, and me to a summer church camp at Kuttawa Springs, near Kuttawa, Kentucky. I remember how excited we were. We had never been to camp before. There were several cabins in a row on the ridge of a hill and a large swimming pool across the road. I had never been in a pool before.

We walked down the hill every morning after the bugle call to brush our teeth at the bubbling spring that streamed out of the sides of a concrete form.

We found a strange curved brick wall beside the road that had a tree growing on top. It was the remains of an iron smelting furnace. There had been several of these furnaces in that area before the Civil War. When the owners lost their slaves, plus the depletion of timber, this industry slowly collapsed.

Members of the DeGraffenreid and Pritchett families owned the one called Mammoth Furnace, plus ten thousand acres of land. They eventually sold the land in parcels to German immigrants, whom they helped settle in that area.

They also donated land there for a church. All their land is now in the recreational area called Land Between the Lakes. There is a huge hydroelectric plant on the dam that was built to form Kentucky Lake. Lake Barkley now covers Kutawa Springs.

It was on a Memorial Day that I first learned what had happened to Ann's mother. We called this Decoration Day and we went with other members of our families to decorate the graves with flowers. I followed Ann and her group around and once when she knelt to put flowers on a grave, she said, "This is where my Mother is buried." I was shocked. I knew something had happened to Ann's mother, but I didn't know she was there in the ground, behind my Sunday School and church.

Miss Delia had several sisters and Ann's mother was not the only one she lost. When they were children their parents had taken them by covered wagon to visit relatives across the Little Wabash River in Illinois. They found that rain had swollen the river. They had the kind of wagon bed that floats like a boat (probably a Conestoga or prairie schooner), so they drove into the river. Ann's Grandma, then Julia (Presley) Poole, was holding Adelia in her right arm and Mary in her left arm. During the struggle with the rushing water, Mary slipped from her mother's arm and was lost in the dark. Her body was later discovered rolled up in quilts and wedged between a chest and the side of the wagon. She had drowned.

During the four years of World War II, Ann and I were in our preteens and were not aware of just how big and far reaching this war was. We heard people talk about it and heard news reports on the radio. Names like Ernie Pyle, a newsman, and McArthur, Eisenhower, and Patton, our generals, and Hitler the mean man who was the cause of it all, became household words.

The war began to hit home when my Uncles Delmer, L.D., and Eugene were drafted. Then Ann's cousins, Ivan and Kenneth, had to go. The big blow came when we learned Ivan had been taken prisoner by the Germans. His fiance, Lucy Powell, took a job with Mr. Roy at the bank and moved in with the Russells.

I saw her walking back and forth to the bank every day. Her head was always down. I thought it was because she was so sad. It could have been that she was watching where she stepped on our crooked, cracked sidewalks. She probably walked around the wavy, roller coaster boardwalk that Ann and I liked to run across.

When Marvin turned sixteen and could drive, he got a job working as a civilian in an Army Ordnance Motor Pool at Camp Breckenridge. He saw German soldiers held prisoner there and wanted to talk to them. He bought a German language book and gave himself a crash course in German. The ones he talked to said they liked it there, because they were safe from the fighting. There are still beautiful murals on the walls in one of the buildings that a German prisoner painted. Marvin didn't wear a uniform until he joined the Army Enlisted Reserve Corps (ASTRP) at age seventeen in 1945. As soon as Mr. Roy and Miss Delia learned Ivan had been captured by the Germans, they went to Camp Breckenridge to consult with officials for the Red Cross and learn how they could write to him. I was invited along.

We had to stop at the entrance to be cleared for entering this strange place. When we were allowed to drive past the guards, I looked out the back window of the car and gave them a big smile. I wanted to reassure them they had not just let a car full of dangerous spies into their military base.

Ann, Mary Ann, and some of our friends formed a Victory club. We wanted to do something to help end the war. There was a drive for citizens to buy U.S. War Bonds. We agreed to each bring a dime to our meetings to buy ten-cent savings stamps that would be glued into a special book. When this book was filled, it could be exchanged for a twenty-five dollar War Bond.

Miss Delia soon put a stop to this project. She came to me, since I was the leader, and wanted to know whose name would go on this bond. I didn't know a name had to be on it. I had not looked far enough ahead to realize the bond could be cashed some day. I just wanted to get this money to the soldiers to help them stock up on bullets and get rid of Hitler.

This point in my story gives me a good opportunity to tell you about Miss Delia. If I should ever make a list of unforgettable Kentucky personalities, she would definitely be on it. I have always liked, admired, and respected her, but I could easily come unglued in her presence. Part of this could be due to the fact she was a school teacher and demanded perfection.

She seemed so perfect to me. When I was near her I would wonder, "Is my hair combed? Is my dress clean? Am I using correct English?" I would imagine that she was evaluating every move I made and I preferred for Ann to come to my house or Mary Ann's to play. Then I could relax from my self-imposed stress, and just be plain me.

Miss Delia was an elegant, ambitious lady. To the end of her days she worked on her education and self improvement. No one could mistake this woman for a Kentucky hillbilly. There were several women in town who were intelligent, with endearing qualities that made them ladies, but they fell into different degrees of elegance. There were the motherly Aunt Bea types, the classy Donna Reed types, and the Regal types. Miss Delia was in the latter group. In my child's mind, I had elevated her to a notch below Queen Victoria, and that lower rank was only because she didn't have a title.

Miss Delia was strict, but she was also a very caring person. I remember one day when Mama was on an all-day shopping trip. She had left a full meal on the table for the older children, who could stay home alone. I went to Ann's that morning to play. At noon Ann was called in to eat. I went home and looked the food over, but I either wasn't hungry or was in a hurry to get back to playing and didn't eat a bite.

Roy and Adelia Russell's house in 1993

I waited for Ann at the big tree near the road at the end of the driveway. When Ann came out, Miss Delia was with her and she walked all the way across that big yard to where I was and asked, "Dorothy have you had any dinner?" (She knew Mama was out of town.) I didn't tell her there was food at home and I didn't want to eat. I just answered her question and said, "No."

She marched me into her back porch to the washstand and told me to wash my hands while she went into the kitchen and dished up a plate of food. The back porch was screened, with a well in the corner of a grey enameled wooden floor. Although this house was one of the newest and most modern in town, plumbing and a bathroom were still in the future.

Their old house had burned to the ground and Miss Delia told us how Cousin Roy had been able to carry out the refrigerator and save it. In times of stress, people sometimes have a burst of super-human strength. She also told of looking at the charred ruins and seeing the thick pile of ashes in the corner of what had been their bedroom. "That was a pile of beautiful quilts I had stacked in a chair. I just stood there and cried," she said.

Miss Delia took me and my clean hands and her plate of food straight through the kitchen into the dining room. She seated me at their big, shiny, varnished dining table. The kitchen had a small, white enameled wooden table, but the dish pans for washing dishes were on it.

I sat alone in that pretty dining room and ate. I loved the inside of this house. It had hardwood floors, venetian blinds, draperies, and pretty furniture. In the middle of the back wall in the living room was a modern fireplace of light-colored wood. All the old Victorian houses had dark walnut or mahogany mantles. On each side of the fireplace in the corners of the room were doors that led to two bedrooms. To the right, beside the door off the front porch, were double french doors that opened into a formal dining room.

Here I sat, like a little princess, being waited on hand and foot, something I wasn't accustomed to, being from a large family. Miss Delia watched from the kitchen to make sure I had eaten every bite on my plate. There was roast beef, potatoes and gravy, a biscuit, and several vegetables. As soon as she saw my plate was empty, she removed it and placed a piece of cherry pie in front of me. This was one of those fleeting moments in life that one never forgets. I felt so important sitting alone in that pretty dining room, while Ann and my Queen Victoria were in the kitchen washing dishes. I enjoyed every minute of it.

Then one day something even more pleasant occurred. Ivan came home from the War. The news spread through town like wildfire and as soon as my family heard, we ran to their house to see him. The yard and porch, where Ivan was sitting, were already filled with people. Ann came out and took me inside. We darted from here to there trying to take in all the excitement. In a quiet town, where a thunderstorm is an event, this was truly one of the biggest events I can remember.

In the kitchen, several women were happily preparing a fancy meal. I saw a relish dish on the cabinet with radishes that had been transformed into roses. I had never seen this done before. I thought it was this magic moment that had given these women the ability to turn radishes into roses.

While I stood there studying them, Miss Delia came back to the kitchen for the umpteenth time, apologizing for running to the porch so often. "I'm sorry," she said, "I just have to see if he is really home. I still can't believe it."

Several years after Ivan and Lucy were married, he became the first principal of the newly consolidated Webster County High School. They built a beautiful home just south of Poole.

Ann, Mary, and I were soon back to normal playing. We played in Mary Ann's yard most often, since it had a big shaded yard and the playhouse Uncle Tom built. Mary shared her roller skates and once when it was her turn, she failed to turn in time and tumbled down the long flight of concrete steps. She crawled back up covered in bad scratches and tears.

We played games such as Go In and Out the Window, Ring Around the Roses, London Bridge, Simon Says, and Hide and Seek. We roamed the garden, picking and eating strawberries, gooseberries, and grapes.

Once we made a mud pie on an old round stove lid, then decorated it with green grapes. It looked so good, Uncle Tom gave it to his neighbor, Rex Cason, for his birthday. The man cut a piece to eat before he discovered he had been tricked. Some of our pies were in fruit jar lids and decorated with dandelions. These delicacies were not digestible, but if appearance counted, they were fit to set before the king.

Miss Delia had Uncle Tom finish her large attic. He papered it all with pretty flowered wallpaper and put wall-to-wall linoleum on the floor. There was also an alcove in front behind the dormer windows. All this open space was the biggest bedroom I had ever seen. Miss Delia let Ann have a slumber party when it was finished. There were four or five girls in two double beds.

We talked and giggled far into the night. Finally, Miss Delia was forced to come upstairs and have a talk with us before we were willing to settle down in the thick feather beds, under homemade quilts, and go to sleep.

In those days, no one went out of town very often. Spending the night with a friend was a special pleasure and we did it quite often.

Our town was small, but there was always plenty to do. We went to ball games, pie and burgoo suppers, plays, Halloween and Christmas parties, and church socials.

Younger children seldom had birthday parties until they were sixteen, but often there would be a big birthday dinner for an older person. The half of the town that was most closely related would be there. That is why they were always referred to as "a big birthday dinner."

We always looked forward to Christmas. Ann and I exchanged our gifts early. Our families didn't celebrate together like Mary and I did at our grandmother's house.

I remember one gift from Ann was a tall round box of bath powder, another was a pretty picture of a girl in an old-fashioned dress. I gave this picture to my first daughter-in-law, Diane.

One Christmas Eve day, Ann came down to my house to show me her new white cowgirl boots. She said Santa had left an early gift for her. We both wondered why he had not left an early gift for me too.

When Ann came to my house to play we often made chocolate fudge. When the candy cooled, we cut it into squares and ate it. We thought it was very delicious in spite of the fact it was often more sugary than creamy.

In these long ago days, girls didn't have many dolls and they often used a little sister to dress up and play with. Anna Lorene and I would sometimes put a big dress on Linda, stuff it full of old clothes until she was round as a ball, then stand back and laugh as she gleefully stumbled around. She would usually fall down and lie there waving her arms and legs like a helpless bug on its back, and be at our mercy until we decided to put her on her feet again.

One summer day, Ann and I decided to play with Linda and dress her up like a doll. She was hot and dirty, so we wanted to give her a bath first. We took her into Ann's screen-enclosed back porch, where the water well and wash pans were. We took off all her clothes. While we were busy getting the water ready, Linda decided not to be a doll and played Lady Godiva instead. She slipped out the back door. By the time we found her, she had already crossed the road and was streaking down the sidewalk, wearing nothing but a silly grin.

Ann and I chased after this two legged slab of naked flesh, never able to close the gap of several feet between us. Linda looked back at us as she ran, a gleeful expression on her face, like the runaway gingerbread boy in our story books. That face had a triumphant look that said, "Ha! ha! catch me if you can."

Fortunately it was not far from Ann's house to mine, but there was still enough time for the occupants of a few out-of-state cars to see this spectacle and wonder about life in a small town.

These travelers through our town sometimes got other surprises. Ann and I loved to pick the long-stemmed white clover that grew so profusely in our yards. We fashioned necklaces, bracelets, and crowns by tying these little white flower balls together. One day we made a chain so long it would reach across the road. It gave us an idea for a new use for our craft. Ann stood on the bank, on the Tapp's side of the road, holding one end. I stood under the only oak tree in the row of locusts on our side, holding the other end. This was the highest point on our bank. Although this was Highway 41 and a major north-south artery, it was only a narrow two lanes wide and sufficient to carry the light traffic back then.

Linda

Cars slowed to about twenty miles per hour through town. This gave us time to raise the chain to the height of the windshield long enough to see startled expressions on faces, then we lifted it higher to clear the car. Sometimes we weren't fast enough and an antenna would catch our chain. We then saw a piece of our work go flying down the highway, still attached like a little flag. We gathered the remaining chain, repaired it, and were soon back at work, terrorizing our unsuspecting victims.

When we grew tired of this we might decide to go bobsledding. Lack of snow was no obstacle. The banks in front of our houses were almost straight up and down. All we needed for a sled was a tow sack. This was a coarse woven sack of tough, brown cloth that feed came in. We sat on the sack at the top of the hill, one in front of the other. The driver would grab hold of one end of the sack and grip tightly to keep it from slipping backwards. Then with a shove of our feet, we would go sledding and bumping to the bottom. We could feel every lump in the hillside, but that only increased the thrill of our ride.

Eventually we grew up and graduated from high school. I had started to school a year ahead of Ann, but I dropped out after my sophomore year when I got married. A year later, I decided I wanted to return to school. This put me in Ann's class and we graduated together.

Ann married one of our teachers, the tall, dark, and handsome Bill Johnson. We both moved to Evansville and lived on the same side of town. We visited often. One day when I went to her house, I found Bill had left for Texas. He had not been able to get his teacher's contract renewed so had gone to stay with relatives there and look for work.

Two weeks later, I returned for another visit and saw all her curtains down. I knocked on the door - no answer. She had moved to Texas, I later learned from Mary Ann. We never wrote. A short time later, Ann came home for a class reunion. After that I didn't see her again for about thirty years. Her husband Bill was on the Dallas police force when President John F. Kennedy was assassinated.

One day last summer, I heard doors shut in my driveway. I looked out and saw Mary Ann and a strange woman coming toward the door. "That must be Ann," I thought. I knew she was visiting in Poole and Mary had said she might bring her by. We both were heavier, with greying hair. If we had passed each other on the street we would simply have walked on by.

After we sat in the living room for a while, talking and laughing and remembering the good old days, I began to see signs of the young, slender girl with the big blue eyes and short black curls that I had grown up with. She was still living inside this woman, who seemed almost like a stranger. I felt warm and happy. I was so glad she had come for a visit.

Ann

RAINBOWS AND DREAMS

One of the best things about living in the country with so many friends and relatives was the frequent invitations to visit in their homes, sometimes for a whole week at a time. A fondly remembered time happened the summer before I started to school.

Mama packed a big, brown paper sack with clothes for me. That Sunday night after church, I went home with my second cousin, Louise Allen. Her father, Everett (Mama's first cousin), was the son of Aunt Hattie and Uncle Bloom Allen mentioned in the first story. Her mother, Ruby Newton Allen, was the girl with the kind of ruby engagement ring Mama wanted.

Louise, with her short blonde curls, was four years older than I. She was the nearest I ever came to having a big sister. Since I was the first girl in our family and the first granddaughter on both sides, I only had younger sisters and cousins to play with.

The Allens lived in a farmhouse, just two or three miles southwest of Poole. I will never forget that week. I will never forget how much fun I had and how good Louise was to me. She was so sweet and pretty, I wanted to be just like her. She only had an older brother, so she probably enjoyed having a chance to play the role of big sister.

That first night, as we lay in bed in the darkened room, she told me not to be afraid of that large "scary looking thing" we could see in the moonlight outside the window. "It is only an old burned tree trunk that was left after the tree was struck by lightning," she said.

First thing next morning, Louise unpacked my sack of clothes and chose a little cotton print dress for me to wear, but it was too wrinkled to suit her. She heated a flat iron on the cookstove and ironed my dress on the kitchen table.

After breakfast was over and the dishes were done, she gave me a manicure. Then we went outside to two large trees near the back porch. A hammock made with curved barrel staves hung between the trees. We swung in it awhile, listening to the songbirds.

Under one tree was her outdoor playhouse. She had odds and ends of boards and boxes for furniture, as well as cracked dishes and fruit jar lids to make mud pies in. We decorated the pies with flower petals.

She taught me how to make fried chicken. "Gather some twigs and break them into short pieces," she said. "Make sure some have big bumps and some have forked branches. Now dip them in water and roll them in the thick dust under the hammock." We soon had a tempting (or maybe not) platter of chicken wings and drumsticks, fried to a crisp drab shade of mud brown.

Another day we gathered eggs and explored everything from the hen house to the outhouse. I saw an apple tree nearby and picked an apple. I started to take a bite when Louise said, "That apple is too green. If you eat it you will be sick and I will have to give you a dose of castor oil." Yuk. I knew all about castor oil. Mama thought it cured just about anything. I threw the apple down.

We went back into the house. On the back porch stood a strange metal contraption I had never seen before. "That is a cream separator," Louise explained. "We pour fresh milk into it and it separates the cream from the rest of the milk. The white, watery skim milk is fed to the hogs. We use the cream to make butter, or we can sweeten it to use on peaches or cereal. If there is more than we need we put it in large cream cans and sell it."

One day it rained and we climbed the narrow stairs to a roomy, floored attic. Louise pulled out a big flat dress box and opened it. Inside was her paper doll collection, cut from Sears catalogs. We played for hours with these tiny families of people and their clothes and possessions, while the rain drummed on the rooftop.

Later in the afternoon the rain ended. We went outside to fresh, clear air and the clean, cool, soft stillness that settles over farmland in the evening.

Louise's father came out of the house to go find the cow and bring her home to milk. We walked with him as far as the pasture gate. We climbed on top to sit and wait and look at the freshly-washed pasture. Blades of grass and wildflowers glistened with tiny drops of water and a rosy glow filled the air. The sound of a cowbell came from near the woods.

Suddenly a beautiful rainbow appeared in the eastern sky. It was a complete half circle touching the earth at each end behind the treetops. I don't think I have seen such a perfect and brilliant one since that day when I was five.

Louise broke into my thoughts and informed me, "There is a pot of gold at the end of the rainbow and it belongs to whoever finds it. But no one has ever been able to find it yet." This news amazed me. In my mind's eye, I could see a pot like Mama's old black, three-legged wash kettle filled with gold nuggets the size of eggs.

I decided right then and there that as soon as I was old enough to leave home alone, I would travel until I found it, even if I had to go half way around the world to do it.

Little did I realize that day, sitting on top of an old rickety, grey pasture gate, that I already had something worth more than gold. It was my Kentucky childhood. I lived in a scenic place with beautiful trees, singing birds, and brilliant, sweet-smelling flowers. I had fresh air to breath, clean water to drink, and an abundance of wholesome food. I had dozens of friends and family, like my cousin Louise, who loved and cared about me. I had freedom and peace.

When all the excesses of life are stripped away, these are the things that are left, these are the things that really count, and they are worth far more than gold.

While finishing this story, it came to me in a flash. I realized I really have, in a sense, found the pot of gold at the end of the rainbow and I didn't need to go half way around the world to do it! The rainbow has been around me all along. We all are, from time to time, under a rainbow. People directly under the cloud from which sunlight reflects to make a rainbow for others can't see it.

As for the pot, Mama recently gave me her old three-legged, black iron kettle. I could fill it with my books of childhood memories and have something worth more to me than the dreamed-about pot of gold.

Dreams can come true.

Louise visiting our family shortly before Marvin left for the Army - 1945.

POOLE REFLECTIONS

Through smiles and tears along the years,
I sometimes pause to view
A mind's eye full of yesterday
Still bright as morning dew.

From Locust blooms to crowded rooms,
To hay-stacks, tumbling down,
We ran and played the whole day through
Till stars engulfed our town.

We fished for fun, swam our ponds
And flew our kites in March
(born from sticks and Sunday news,
And Mother's home-made starch.)

We milked the cows, hitched-up the mules,
Pulled water from our wells;
Plowed the ground, attended schools
And listened for the bells.

We roamed the town and hurried down
For what the mail did bring,
Then played ball games on pasture green
And sang, like birds in spring.

Hunting rabbits, wading streams,
Picking berries and salad greens,
Cutting weeds, dreaming dreams,
Singing Carols and crowning Queens ---

But I remember most of all
From hills of memories piled,
Those twinkled eyes of elders
Smiling friendly to a child.

Marvin Russell

Billy and me on the Brown farm - 1949. Our marriage in 1948 marked the end of my Kentucky childhood and the beginning of a new life.

Bob under the Locust trees - 1953. Background old smoke house and site of the Brown / Russell house.

Mama and me on Brown farm - 1949. Porch to corncrib were first steps of her runaway route in 1926.

ABOUT THE FAMILY

Although many of the Brown and Russell descendants have moved away from the Poole area, the properties described in the book are still owned and lived on by members of these families.

Years ago Daddy bought two farms that joined the Russell farm east of Dixon. His and Mama's love of the country drew them back to farm life. They cleaned up an old log house on the Cobb farm to live in while their beautiful new brick house was under construction in 1953. It was built with timber cut from tall trees that grew on these farms.

They lived there more than 30 years before moving back to Poole in 1987 to a smaller house near Jimmie. He is the only one of their children who made Poole his permanent home. He took over the garage business when Daddy retired.

Marvin became a scientist, college dean, and university professor. Anna Lorene became a registered nurse, and Linda and I chose the traditional roles as homemakers plus a variety of other occupations. The five of us gave our parents 18 grandchildren. Our family that began with two people now numbers 70.

Christmas Day, 1993, Mama celebrated her 86th birthday. In January she became ill and began longing for her parents. She said, "I want to go home to see Mama and Papa. It has been so long since I have seen them." During the early morning hours of January 24th, while she seemed to be peacefully sleeping, she slipped away from us to join her Mama and Papa, Dallas and Estelle, in another place somewhere beyond the sunset. Mama didn't live to see the finished book, but she had read all the stories and loved them.

Daddy gave me Mama's ruby ring. When I look at it, I am reminded of a lifetime of loving and caring for her family through seven generations, from her great grandmother in the log cabin to her great grandchildren.

Daddy, at 93, still shows his magic tricks. He also entertains the early birds, waiting at the post office for their mail, with his newest joke for the day. He misses Mama but he is a survivor. Sometimes he sings old songs to his grandchildren that his Pappy sang to him many years ago.

The high moral principles and values that were taught to our parents are being passed on to our own descendants, and this good way of life, like a river, flows onward.

My head is filled with more stories, but I have kept the promise I made in the introduction. I gave you a peek into a little town in Kentucky in the simpler days of long ago.

Over the years modern technology brought more changes and a faster-paced life to my hometown, but the kindhearted neighborliness of its people remains.

Acknowledgements

This book would never have been finished without the help of the following people:

First, I want to give heartfelt thanks to my parents for their patience in answering what must have seemed, at times, to be an endless barrage of questions.

A very big thanks goes to my oldest son, Robert, for the long, tedious hours he spent at the computer and for pushing me to write more stories. Additional thanks goes to his son Rob for artwork.

A deeply felt gratitude to my brother, Dr. Marvin Russell, for helping with the facts about our family history and assisting with the chores of editing.

Thanks to my brother, Jimmie, for not shooting down the stories that made him look bad, and to my sisters, Anna Lorene and Linda, for their laughter, encouragement, and story contributions.

Special thanks to Kenneth Russell for the historical accuracy in parts of "My Friend Ann," to sons David and John for tramping around in the bushes for current photographs, and to John and David's wife Susan for additional computer work.

I will never forget the encouragement I received in the nice letters from Dr. and Mrs. B.F. Brown, Frankfort, KY; Lorena Gould, Houston, TX; Dorothea Wells, Monett, MO; Robin Hubbard, Evansville, IN; and Dicie H. Eagan, L.A., CA.

Thanks to Kerry J. Smith for the editing work done in preparing for the second printing of this book.

Finally, a special acknowledgement for my friend, Mrs. Mattie Lou Blackburn. She was the first to hear many of the stories as I read them to her over the phone. Her enthusiastic response would often give me the courage I needed to plow back into a jumble of notes and papers and try to make them readable.

Made in the USA
Charleston, SC
23 August 2012